WHAT YOU NEED

These Wildstyle Graffiti Projects are made with Jumbo Popsicle Sticks. You can buy them by the box at a craft, hobby or art supply store, or on the Internet. They have a smooth finish and are easy to draw and paint on.

Make your projects as simple or complex as you like. Draw basic outline letters or advanced three-dimensional Wildstyle letters. It's up to you! The drawing instructions included on each alphabet page can be adjusted to fit any style of letter. Use my words or make up your own.

MATERIALS NEEDED

- Jumbo Popsicle Sticks
- Tacky Glue (thicker and stronger than white glue) or Multi-Purpose White Glue
- Masking Tape or Blue Temporary Tape
- #2 Pencil
- Pink Eraser
- Ultra Fine Point Sharpies
- Mod Podge or Varnish
- Paintbrush
- Rhinestones or Sequins for highlights

OPTIONAL

- Acrylic Paints & Brush
- Colored Pencils
- Crayons
- Magic Markers
- String (yarn, hemp, rawhide, or any other kind)
- Air-dry Clay (you can buy this inexpensively at a craft store)
- Wire Cutter
- Pair of Scissors
- Ornaments: Shells, buttons, clay, toothpicks, silk leaves, felt, craft foam, gemstones, rhinestones, sequins, rocks, party favors, miniature flowers, beads, wiggly eyes, paper, and plastic stickers, office supplies, wood cutouts, paper clips, magnets, etc.

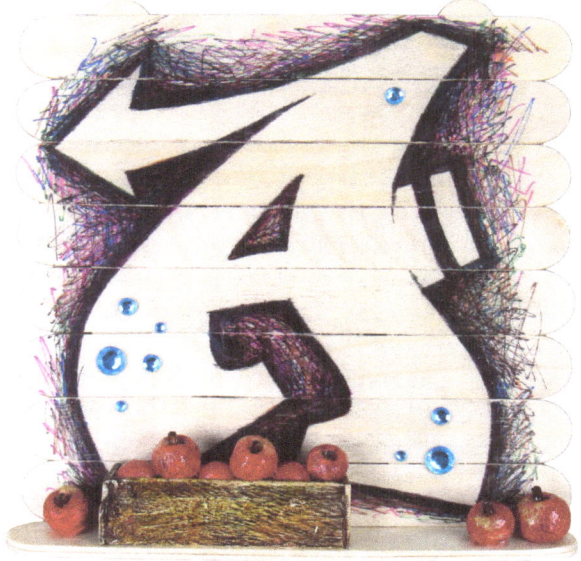

The Alphabet projects featured in this book are colored with Ultra-Fine Point Sharpies which are permanent magic markers. They are water-resistant. But you can use any other tools you like.

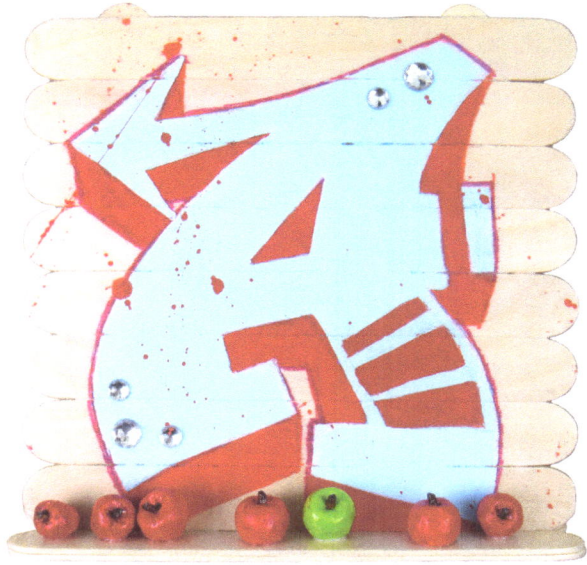

This three-dimensional Wildstyle project is colored with acrylic paint, colored pencils and magic markers. You can use any one or all of these to decorate your projects.

PART ONE: DRAWING LETTERS

Wildstyle is a type of graffiti lettering in which simple outline letters are turned into complex, ornate forms with the addition of elements such as arrows, serifs, extensions, and bits.

Wildstyle was invented by graffiti writers in New York City in the 1970s. Some modern Wildstyle letters are so complicated they are almost impossible to read, but the letters in this book are based on old-school styles which are simpler and easily recognizable.

There is one essential rule you need to follow when creating any Wildstyle letter. The structure of the letter must remain intact. That means an A must look like an A no matter how much you distort the shape of the letter or how many extra elements you add to it. That goes for all letters in the alphabet. Somewhere, some-place, deep down at the core of a Wildstyle letter there has to be the basic structure of the original letter.

With that essential rule in mind, you can create all of the stylish, unique, and exciting Wildstyle letters that your imagination can dream up.

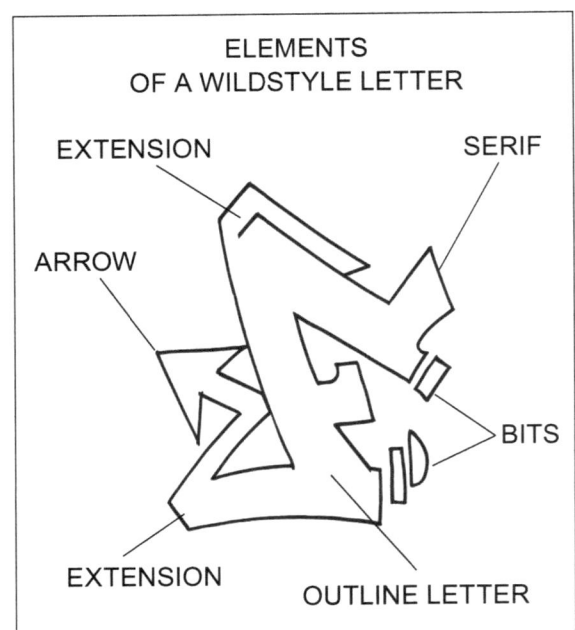

ELEMENTS
OF A WILDSTYLE LETTER

EXTENSION   SERIF

ARROW

BITS

EXTENSION   OUTLINE LETTER

BUILDING OUTLINE LETTERS WITH BARS: <u>THE PLANK METHOD</u>

This is the most effective method I know of for constructing letters. It works with any kind of letter. Think of the bars as planks of wood that are nailed together at the ends. Imagine pivoting them at angles. Follow the steps.

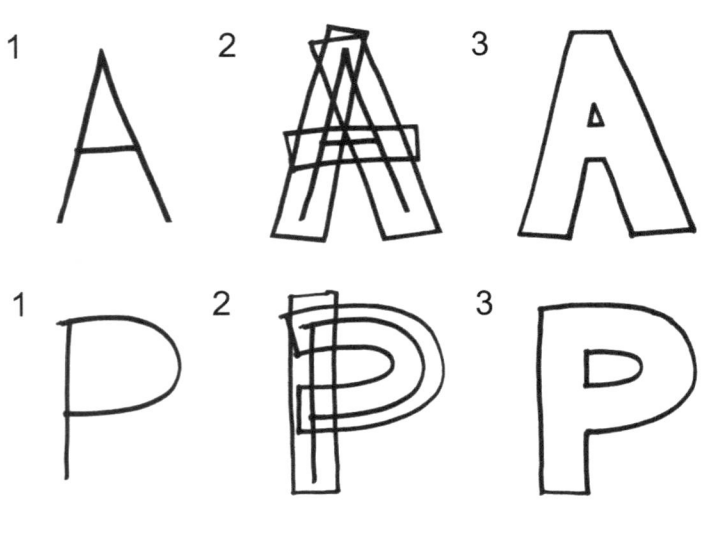

STEP 1. With a pencil draw a basic letter. Keep it simple. Use as few lines (or strokes) as possible.

STEP 2. Draw rectangular bars around the strokes. Overlap the bars at the ends. If a stroke is curved like in the letter P, draw a curved bar.

STEP 3. Draw a dark outline around the outside edges of the letter with a black permanent magic marker such as a Fine-Point Sharpie. Erase the inside lines. **This is your finished outline letter.**

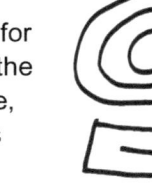

The Plank Method works the same way for every letter. Bend the bars to fit around the shape of the strokes. An S can have one, long curving bar, or several smaller bars connected at the ends.

OR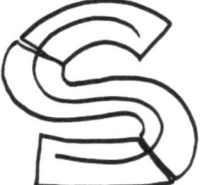

POPSICLE-STICK-GRAFFITI

NUMBER FOUR / DRAW WILDSTYLE

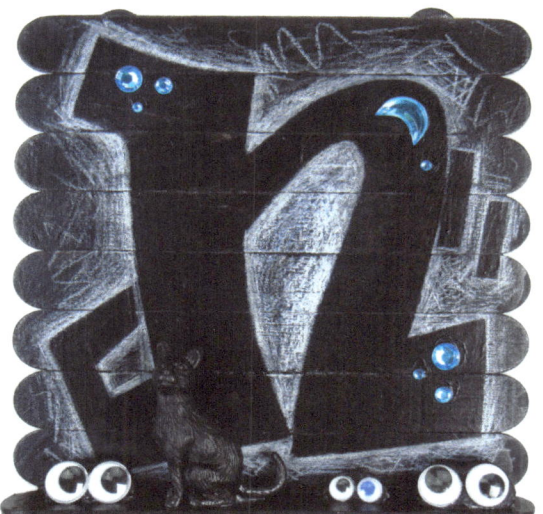

N IS FOR NIGHT

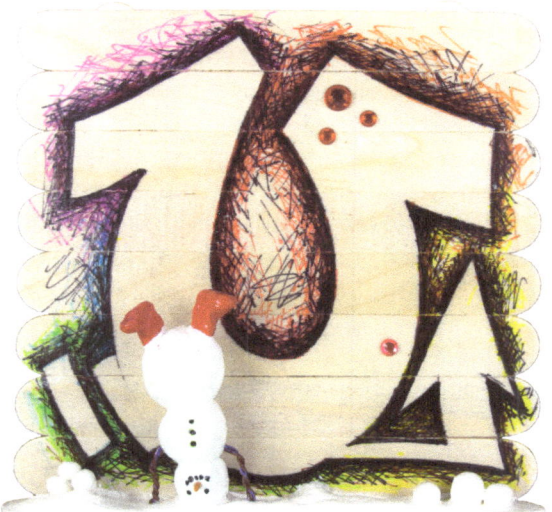

U IS FOR UPSIDE-DOWN

CONTENTS

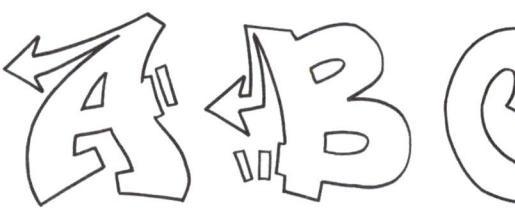

Popsicle-Stick-Graffiti /Number Four/ Draw Wildstyle
First Printing, 2018
ISBN-13: 978-0990438182
Series: Popsicle-Stick-Graffiti ®Published By Graffiti Diplomacy
For general information on our other products, please contact us at "graffitidiplomacy@yahoo.com"
Find us on the web @ graffitidiplomacy.com

ABOUT THIS BOOK

The projects in this book can be scaled up or down for different age groups. For older kids, try three-dimensional letters with acrylic paint. You will find examples in Part Two. Younger children can draw and color simpler letters with markers, crayons, or colored pencils. Any style of letters will work fine. The magic of this project is in the little ornaments added to compliment the letter. An adult can help small ones glue on the little shelf shown on page 20. You don't even need the shelf. Just glue ornaments onto the wood plaque. You don't have to do the project as an alphabet project either. You can use any letter, your name, a word that you like, or a theme such as Christmas. I included a Halloween piece as an example. Collect whatever small ornaments you need that accentuate the letter you choose and glue them on with thick white tacky glue. You can find just about anything you need at a local dollar store or make them yourself with air-dry clay, which can be purchased inexpensively at most craft and art supply stores. After the glue has set, I recommend you paint around the base of the objects with Mod Podge or Varnish to bond all of the pieces firmly together.

More Ideas for Popsicle-Stick-Graffiti Projects:
• A story
• A poem
• A gift for someone with their initial and a few ornaments that represent them
• These projects are easily adaptable for teachers who can assign different words from a lesson plan or theme a class is working on - history, science, nature, literature, math, foreign languages, spelling, geography, politics - all work great with this project!

A FEW WORDS ABOUT ME

Graffiti is a fantastic art form that everyone wants to learn. Graffiti instructional books typically include a section on wall painting. This one does not. Don't get me wrong, I love graffiti of all kinds. I spend my time combing the streets of whatever city or small town I happen to be in, taking photographs of every tag, throw-up, and full-color piece I can locate. Sometimes they are faded and barely visible, painted on smelly dumpsters in restaurant parking lots, or etched onto glass in ancient phone booths with no phones. I love them all.

But my real passion is for the letterforms themselves. And finding interesting ways to apply the letters to surfaces that are legal. This unique approach makes my graffiti instruction guides kid-friendly. And that's a good thing in my opinion. It's a way that everyone can learn to draw graffiti who wants to learn, and apply their newfound skills in ways that are safe and productive. This is a drawing instruction guide, plus an arts & craft project book, and an alphabet book, all rolled into one. It is a book the whole family will enjoy. This book is dedicated to my mom, Elaine Cecily. I love you forever, Mom. ♥

OTHER BOOKS IN THIS SERIES
Popsicle-Stick-Graffiti/ Number Two/ Signs
Popsicle-Stick-Graffiti/ Number Three/ Bubble Letters

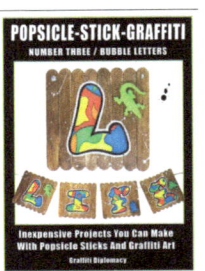

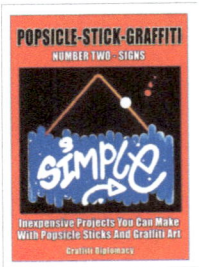

If you want to design your own bubble letters and more styles of graffiti, our two instructional books, "Learn to Draw a Graffiti Master-Piece", and, "Why Write When You Can Tag: Learn To Draw The Best Graffiti Tags Ever!", are a great place to learn graffiti lettering techniques.

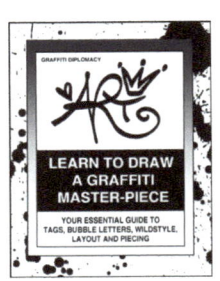

Now try bending a letter. Pull it to the left or right. Stretch it into any shape. First draw the strokes, then put bars around the strokes. Notice how much more animated and lively your letters look when you bend and stretch them in this way.

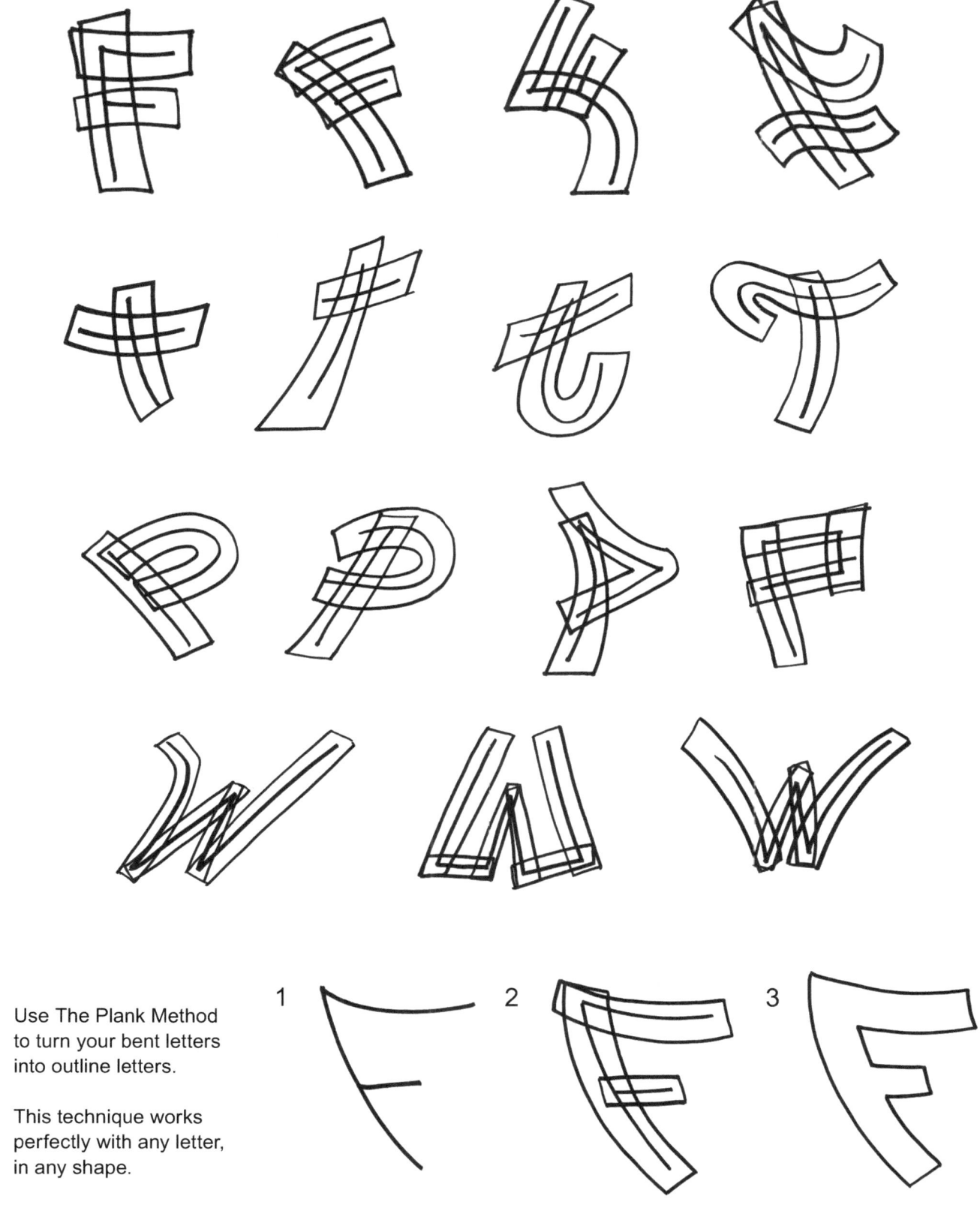

Use The Plank Method to turn your bent letters into outline letters.

This technique works perfectly with any letter, in any shape.

TAG LETTERS

A tag is a graffiti writer's signature. Before there were outline letters there were tags. A tag is drawn quickly with a bit of flair. Over time, with repeated writing, a tag develops characteristics that make it more of a logo than just a simple signature. Creating interesting, eye-catching tags led graffiti writers to the invention of Wild-style graffiti.

Every person's handwriting is unique so the letters that make up a tag are unique as well. There are some general categories we can group tag letters into such as backslanted, round, and square. There are many more styles not listed here.

Tag letters are drawn in a similar way to the bent and stretched letters on page 5. To draw your own tag letters use these three categories (backslanted, round, square) and the bending-stretching technique on page 5 as a guide.

For example, draw a letter F, but stretch it towards the left like a backedslanted letter. Or, draw a K but make it very square and chunky. These are tag letters.

You can find lots more examples of tag letters on the Internet or in books such as my book, "Why Write When You Can Tag: Learn To Draw the Best Graffiti Tags Ever".

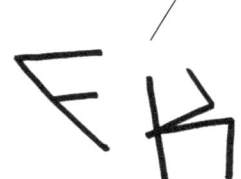

Backslanted

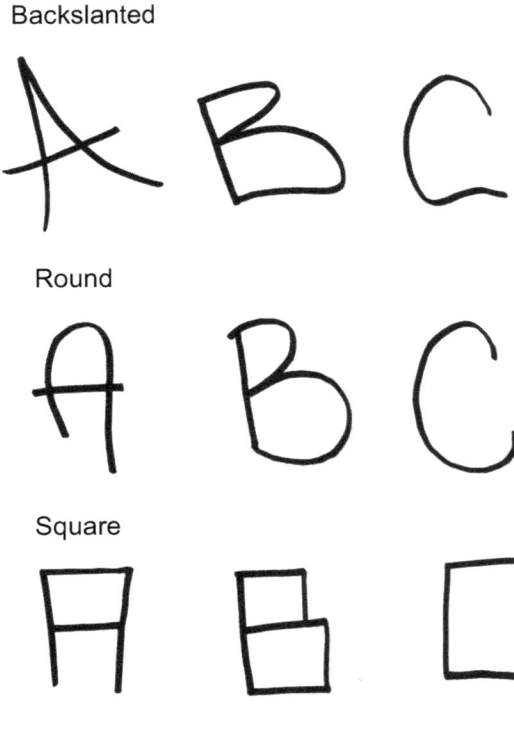

Round

Square

TAG LETTERS WITH SERIFS

SERIFS

Serifs are little flourishes that are attached to the ends of the strokes of some styles of letters. All tag letters can be drawn with serifs or without. Adding serifs to a tag letter makes the letter more interesting, adds balance, plus it provides opportunities to add the extra elements that typically make up a Wildstyle letter.

You can use The Plank Method to turn any tag letter with serifs into an outline letter. It works with any style of tag letter.

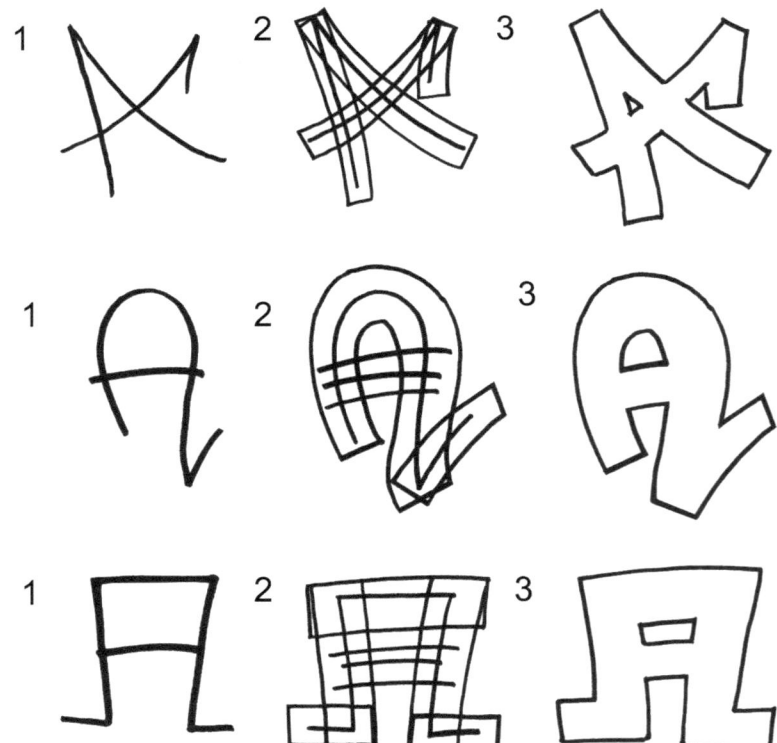

You can stretch out and bend both a tag letter and a serif into any kind of shape that you like. Turn serifs into swirls and loops. Add joints and bend them at sharp angles or make looping, curling squares. There are no set rules.

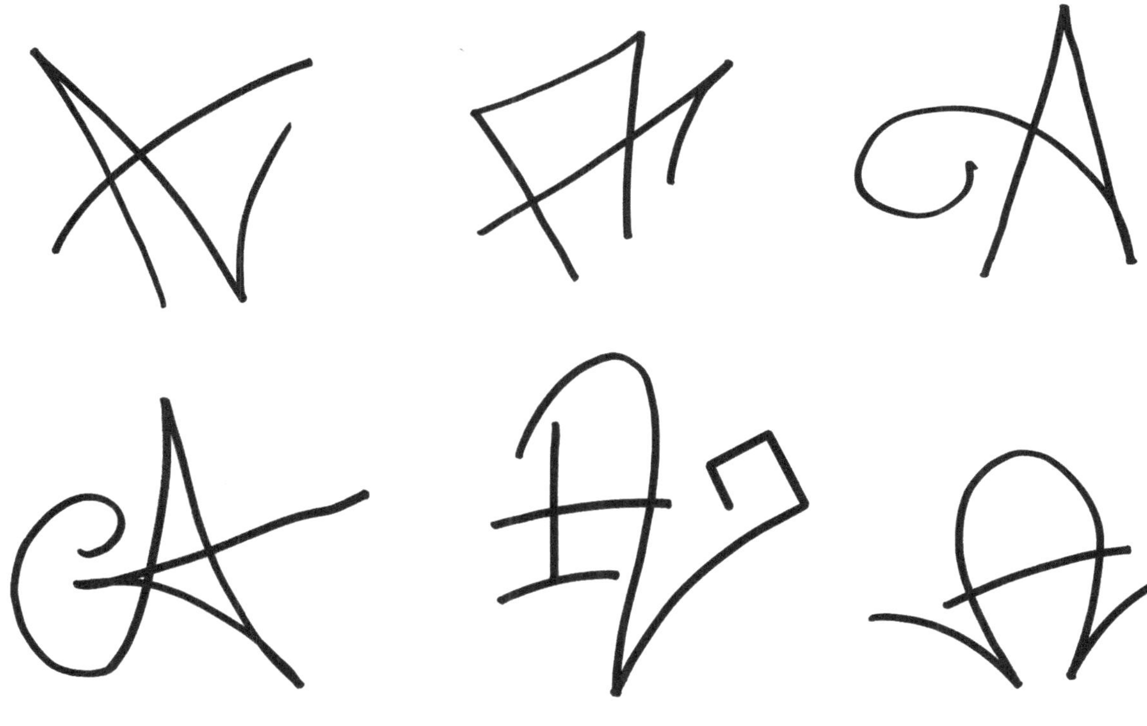

Lowercase letters work the same way as uppercase letters.

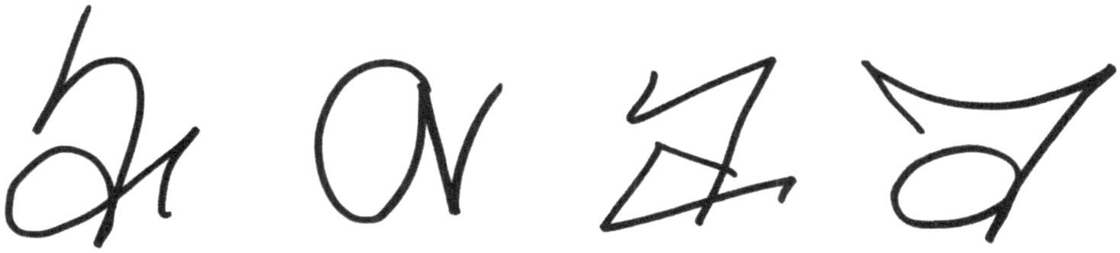

Choose any one of the tag letters above and turn it into an outline letter using The Plank Method. Make sure to put bars around the serifs and follow the twists and curves of the letter strokes.

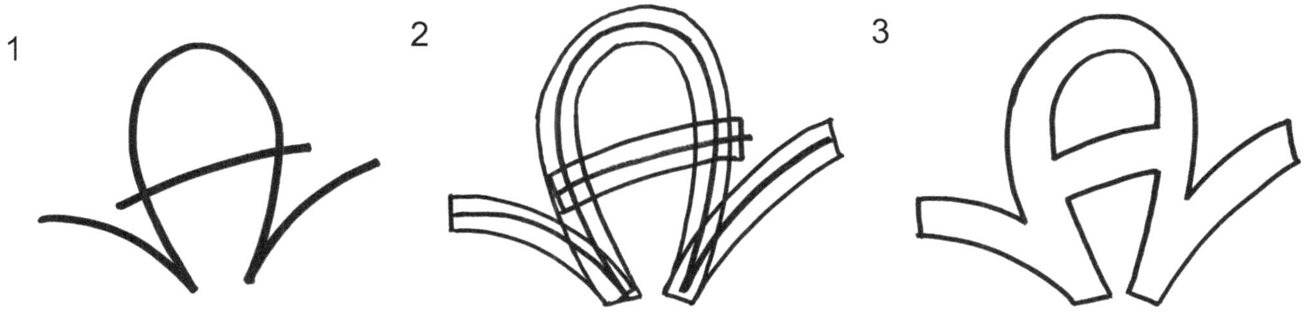

1   2   3

Why are tag letters so important? It turns out if you begin building a Wildstyle letter with a tag letter at its base, you automatically have the foundation for a Wildstyle version of that letter. Pretty amazing. I'll show you how.

ARROWS

Arrows are the most popular additional element added to graffiti tag letters. An arrow can be added to any part of a tag letter in any shape and at multiple points, but arrows work especially well when added to the end of an elongated serif. An arrow should follow the general flow and direction of the strokes of a letter and look balanced to your eye. Practice will teach you where to place arrows for maximum effect.

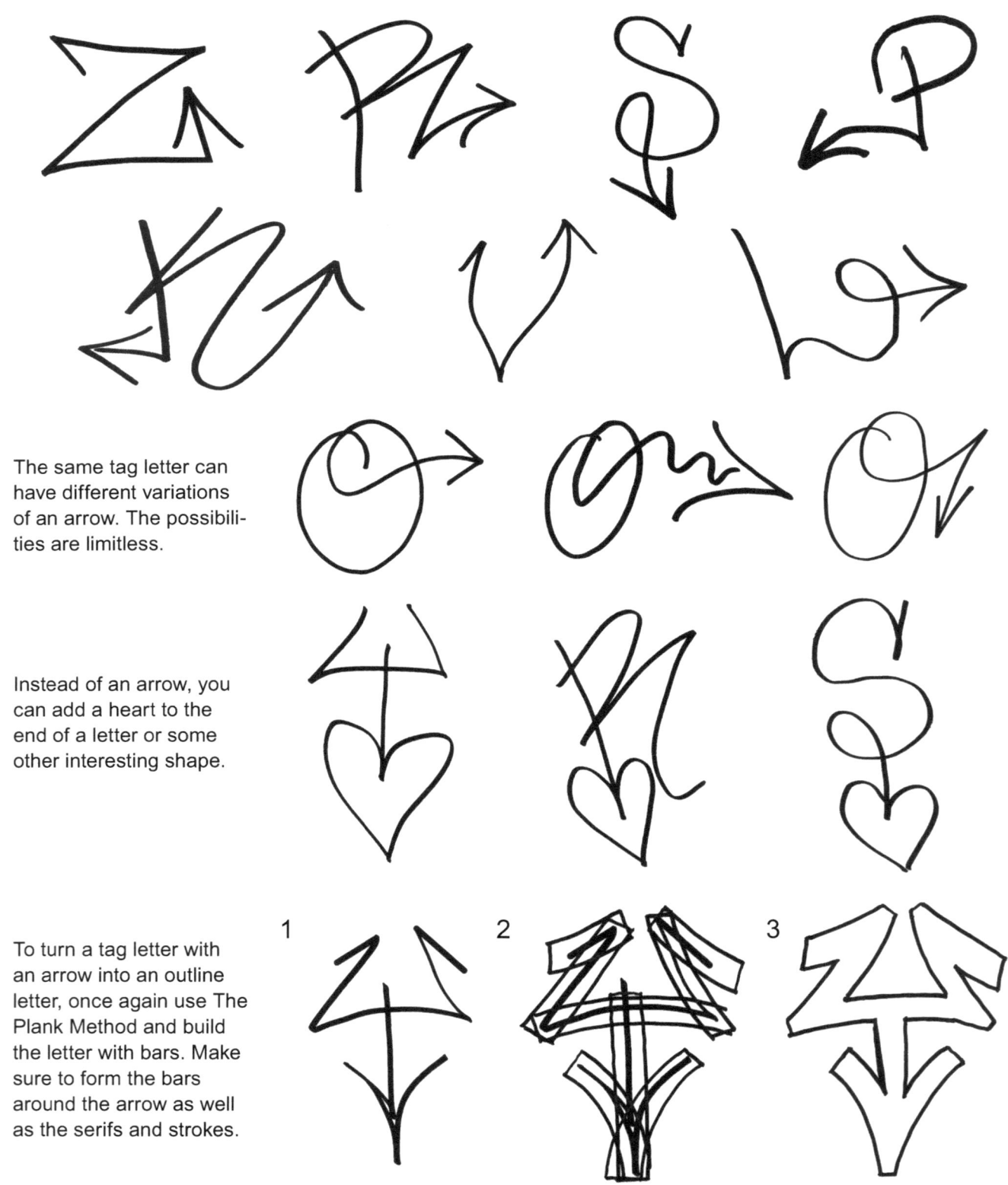

The same tag letter can have different variations of an arrow. The possibilities are limitless.

Instead of an arrow, you can add a heart to the end of a letter or some other interesting shape.

To turn a tag letter with an arrow into an outline letter, once again use The Plank Method and build the letter with bars. Make sure to form the bars around the arrow as well as the serifs and strokes.

EXTENSION

Extensions are extra sections that are added to the foundation of a letter to distort the shape and make the letter more elaborate. With extensions a letter can be enlarged, broken up or diffused in a variety of different ways. The simplest type of extension is an elongated serif with an extra piece added to the end.

You can place serifs on this X in many different positions.

TO CREATE EXTENSIONS:
STEP 1. Elongate one of the serifs.
STEP 2. Use The Plank Method to turn the letter into an outline letter.
STEP 3. Add extra pieces to the end of the serif. In fact, add extra pieces to all the serifs.

You can add extensions anywhere you like. Add arrows at the ends. Bend the extensions or the bars of the letter to change the shape. Add a loop or a swirl to the ends.

Add as many different extra pieces as you want. Notice that you can still make out the original tag letter X underneath no matter how complicated the letter gets.

That brings us back to the original rule: the structure of the letter must always remain intact.

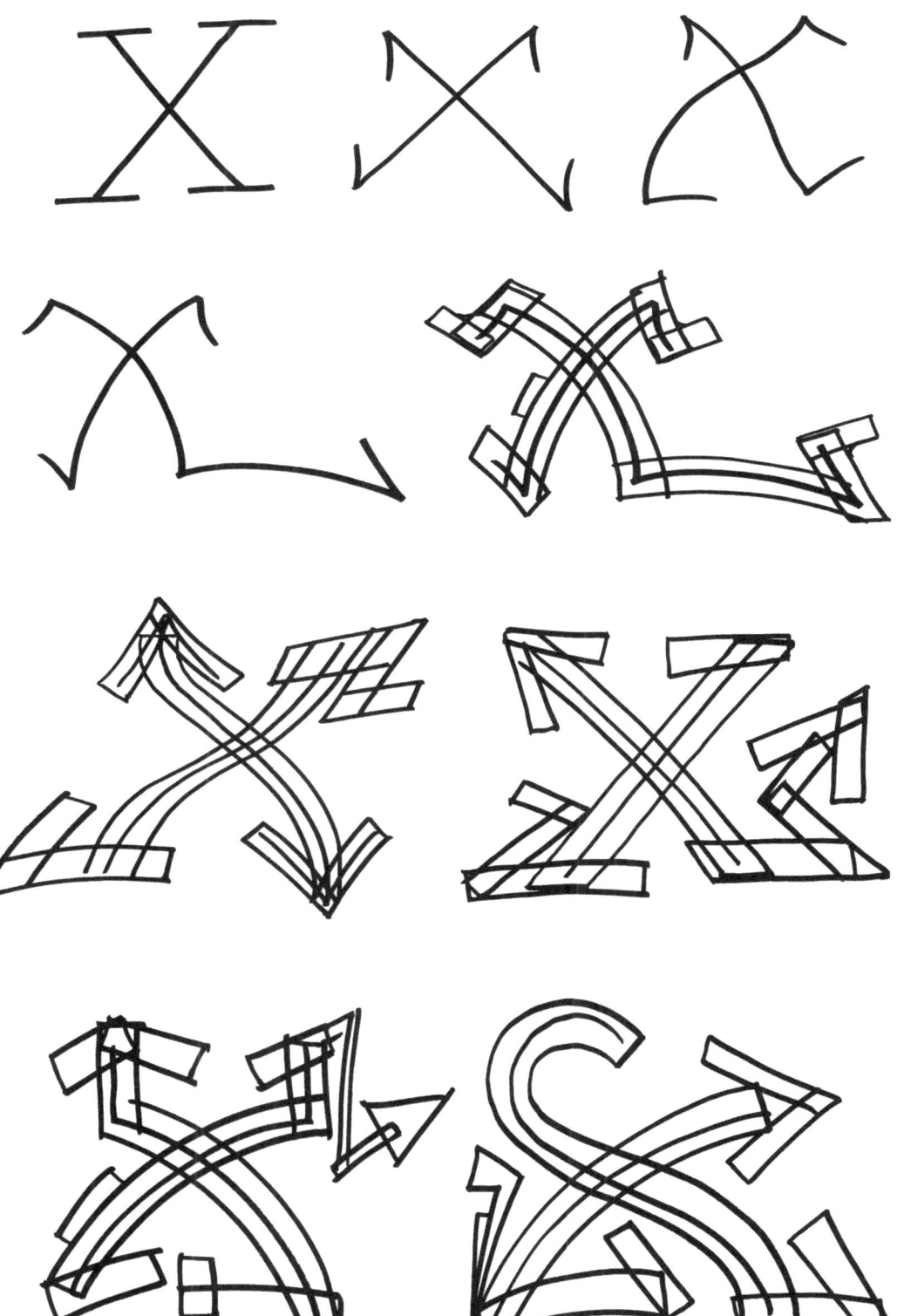

BITS OR CHIPS

Bits are little doodads that have been sliced off from the main body of a letter, an extension or a stroke. They can protrude from anywhere, filling up space, and adding balance and playfulness to the letter.

To create bits, draw an extension, then slice it into sections. Spread the sections out.

Add lots of bits. The ends can be angular or rounded.

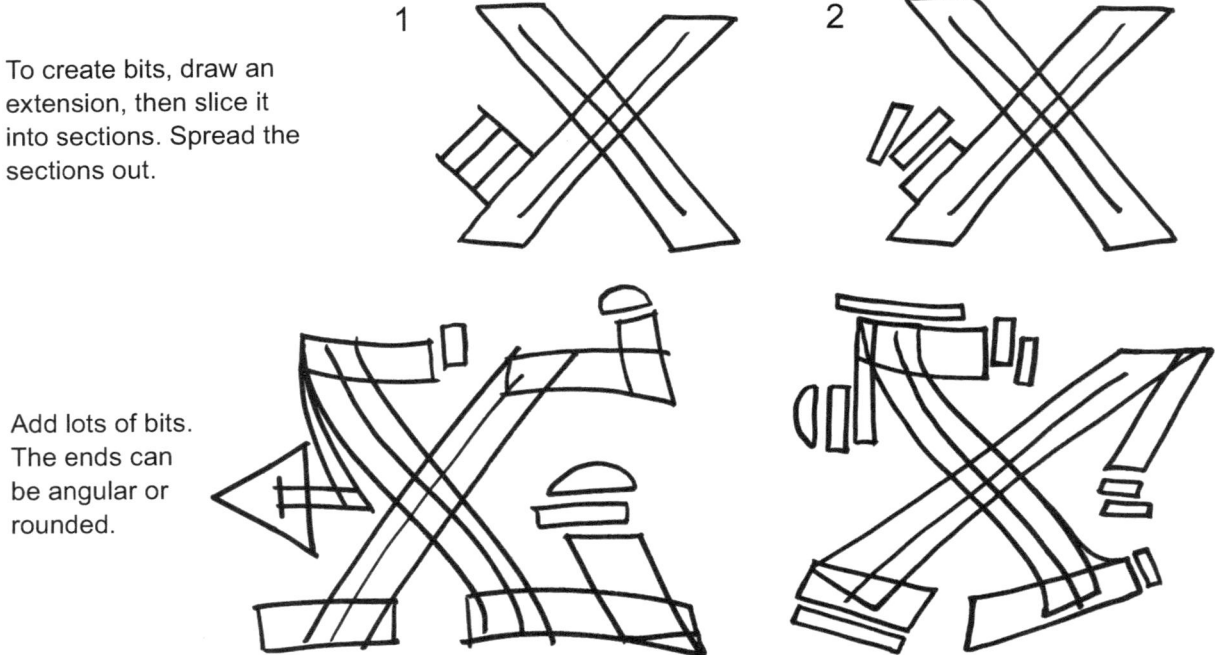

Extensions can originate from any point on a letter, travel any distance, bend, twist and end up at any place outside or even back inside the letter. They can vary in width with thick and thin lines and can finish off with rounded or sharp ends.

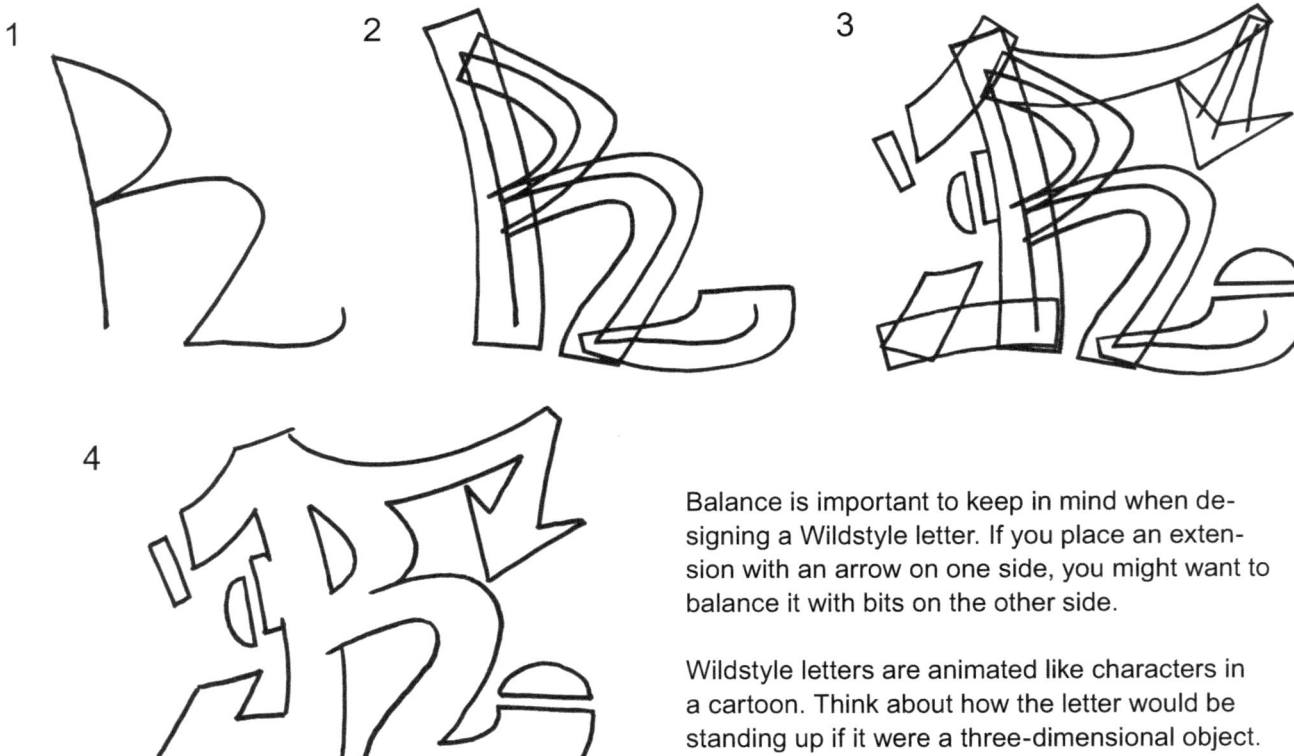

Balance is important to keep in mind when designing a Wildstyle letter. If you place an extension with an arrow on one side, you might want to balance it with bits on the other side.

Wildstyle letters are animated like characters in a cartoon. Think about how the letter would be standing up if it were a three-dimensional object.

So there you have it. To construct a Wildstyle letter, start with a tag letter. Use The Plank Method to turn it into an outline letter. Add serifs, arrows, extensions, and bits. Darken the outline and erase the inside lines.

You can experiment with additional elements to make your letters even more elaborate such as cuts, overlapping pieces, or duplicate sections. Try multiple arrows or star shapes bursting from the side. Eventually, with practice, you can construct your own Wildstyle letters without a tag letter or bars underneath but when you are just starting out this is a great way to learn and develop your skills. I always construct Wildstyle letters this way because it's logical and methodical.

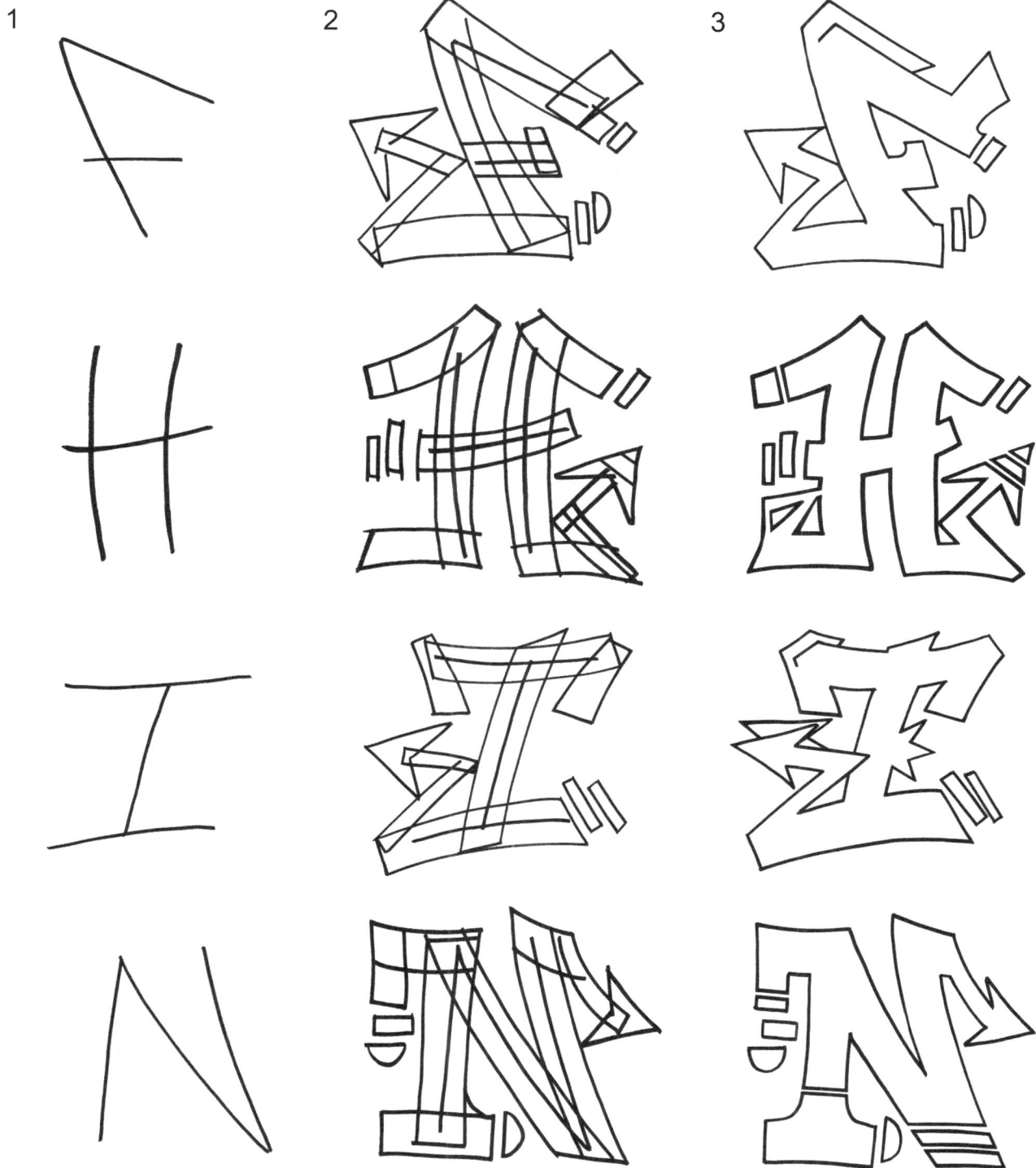

THREE-DIMENSIONAL LETTERS

You can add three dimensions to your letters and give them the illusion of depth. This is called drawing in perspective. Known as 3-D for short, perspective drawing makes an object look life-like. It appears to be floating within a space or standing on a ground, with a top, a bottom or sides. 3-D letters are the most intricate style of graffiti lettering to draw and you don't need to know this technique to make the alphabet projects in this book. But Wildstyle letters often include this advanced drawing style and you can certainly use 3-D letters in your popsicle stick projects to make them into professional looking works of art (see the A project on the bottom of page 3). Here are several different 3-D effects.

BLOCK LETTER

STEP 1. Draw small lines from the edges of the letter, all the same size, and going in the same direction.

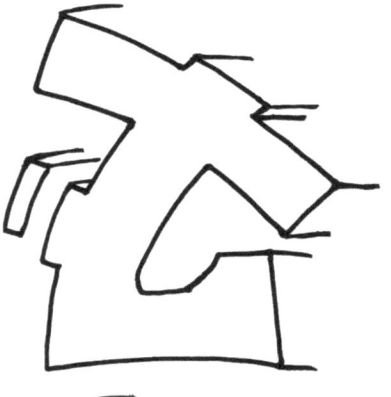

STEP 2. Draw lines connecting the points and following the shape of the letter.

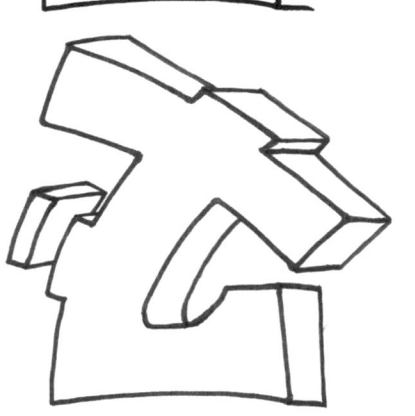

ONE POINT PERSPECTIVE

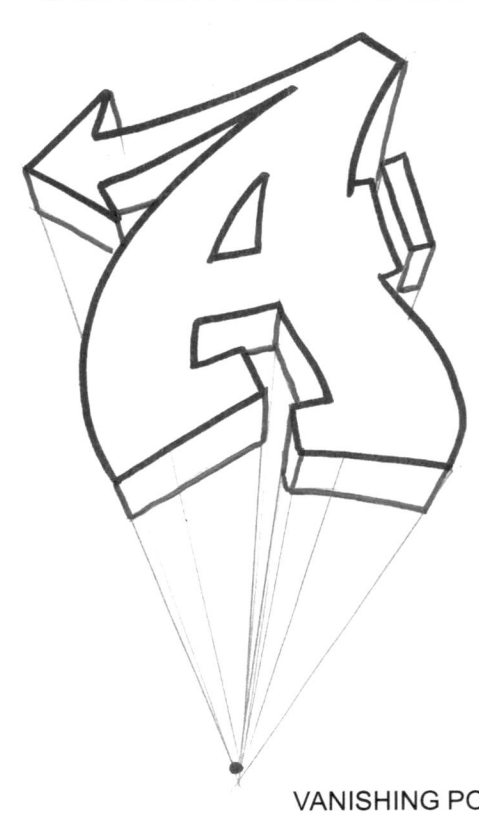

VANISHING POINT

Draw a single point, and draw lines from the point connecting to all the edges of the letter.

DROP SHADOW

Draw a second letter behind the first in any direction to look like the letter is standing in front of its shadow.

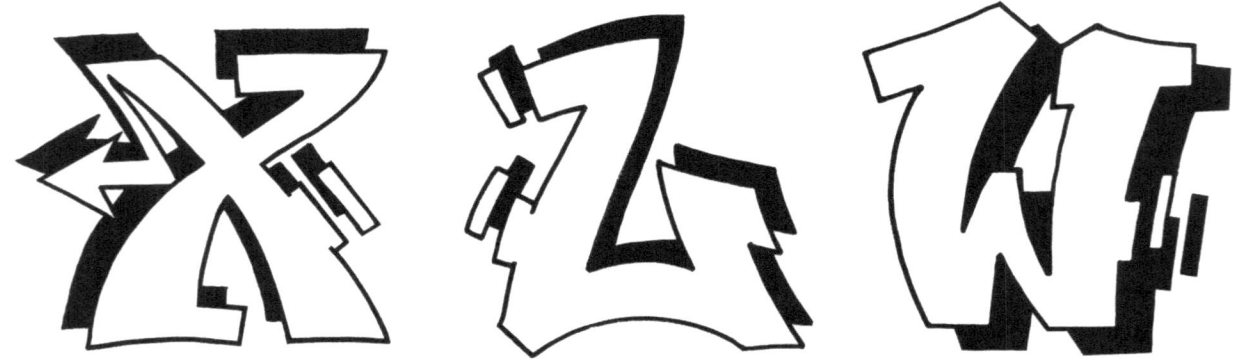

3-D techniques work especially well with Wildstyle letters, accentuating the effects of serifs, extensions, arrows, and bits. Look at the cast shadow of the arrow down on the bottom-right. Very cool! A cast shadow would probably not fit on a popsicle stick project but it's good for you to know about.

BLOCK LETTER

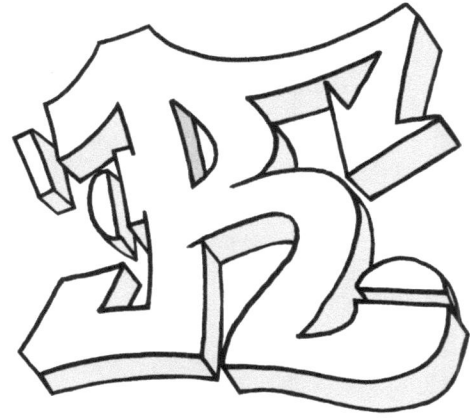

ONE POINT PERSPECTIVE

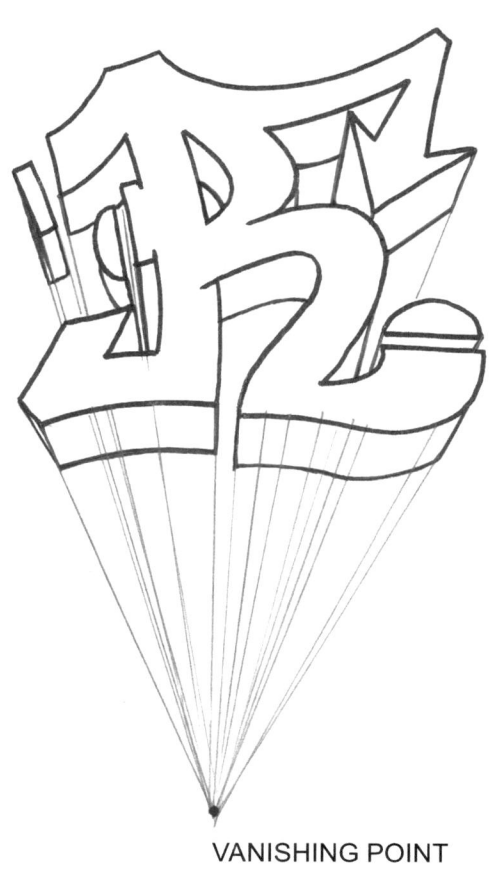

VANISHING POINT

DROP SHADOW

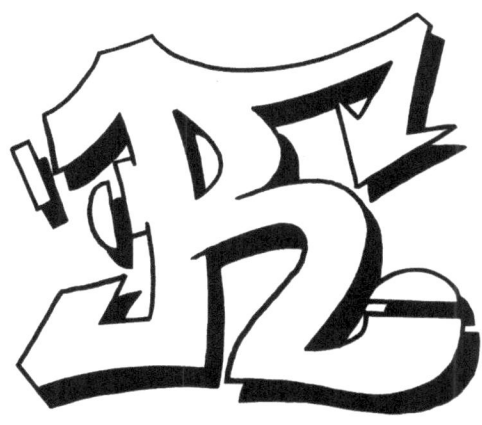

BLOCK LETTERS WITH A DROP SHADOW

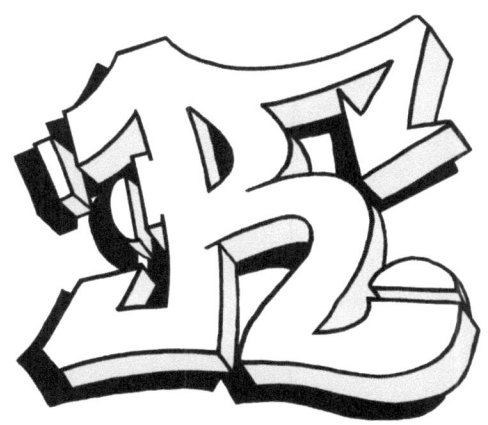

ELONGATED CAST SHADOW

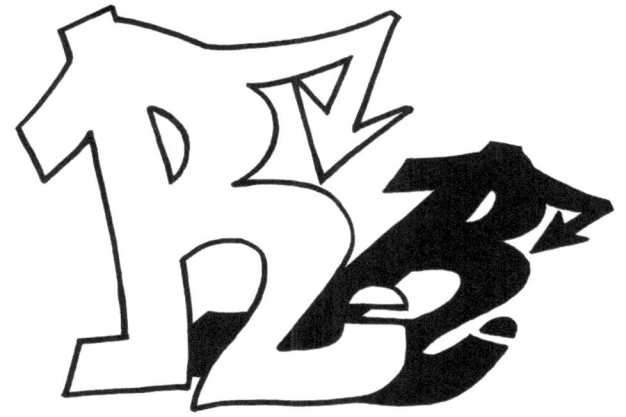

PART TWO: POPSICLE STICK CONSTRUCTION

CONSTRUCTING A PLAQUE

STEP 1. Line up 8 jumbo popsicle sticks.
STEP 2. Glue two sticks onto the back to hold the plaque together.
I recommend using extra thick tacky glue whenever possible to hold the popsicle sticks together, but multi-purpose white glue will work, too. You can buy Tacky glue at your local craft store or art shop.

Extra step: After the glue is dry, you can rub both sides of the plaque with a cool damp cloth, but it's not necessary. This will help seal the wood and make the surface a little easier to work on, plus prevent too much warping, but you have to let it dry overnight. I suggest you experiment and see if you prefer using your wood plaque with or without this extra step.

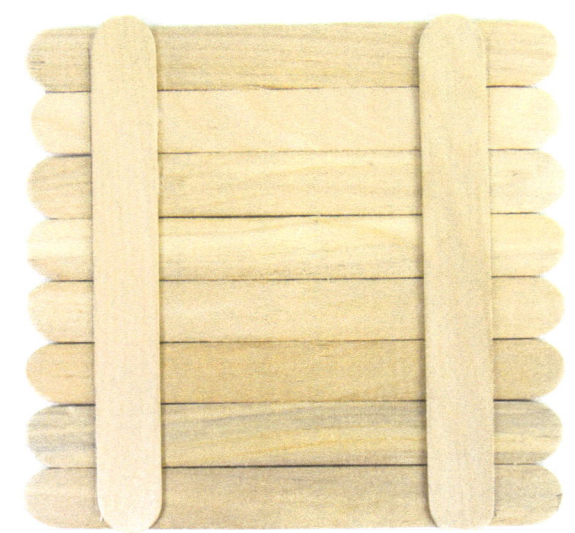

BACK VIEW OF PLAQUE

CONSTRUCTING A SHELF

STEP 1. Glue two jumbo popsicle sticks together. Put them under a book so they dry as flat as possible. Put this shelf aside for later.

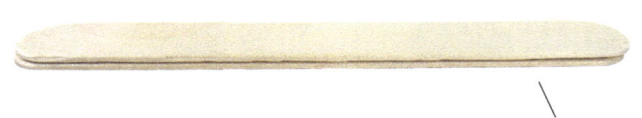

TWO STICKS GLUED TOGETHER

DRAWING A WILDSTYLE LETTER ON THE POPSICLE STICK PLAQUE

STEP 1. Trace the plaque onto a piece of paper. This is where you will practice your drawing skills and work out your design. Sketch out a Wildstyle letter using the diagrams on the alphabet pages 22-47 as a guide. Use The Plank Method. Choose any letter you like to start with.

STEP 2. When you are ready, lightly draw the letter with a pencil onto the front of the wood plaque. Press down very lightly. This will make it much easier to erase the pencil drawing later on. Sketch out the tag letter, then the bars for an outline letter. Add bits.

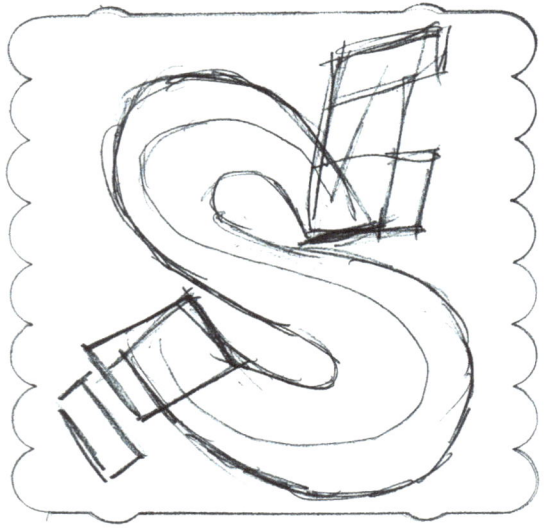

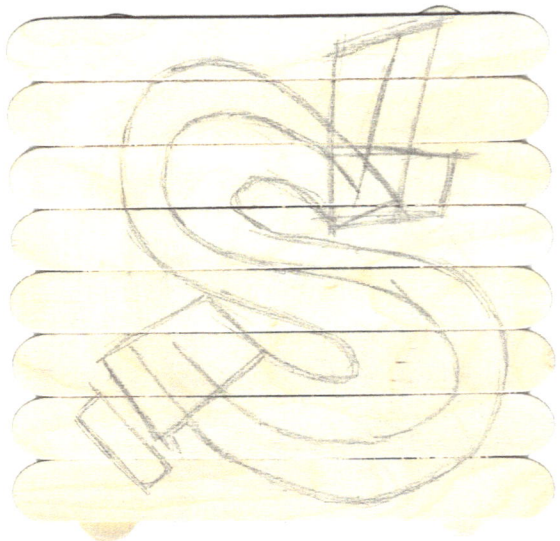

MY SCRIBBLE TECHNIQUE

You can use other methods or tools to color your letters. This is just a technique I like to use. It's fun. Finish with a coat of varnish if you are using colors that don't run. Test your tools before applying Varnish.

STEP 1. Draw a dark outline around the outside edges of the letter with an Ultra-Fine Point Sharpie or some other permanent marker. Erase the inside pencil lines.

STEP 2. With Ultra-Fine Point Sharpies or colored pencils, scribble around the outside of the outline with your choice of colors. I used red and teal.

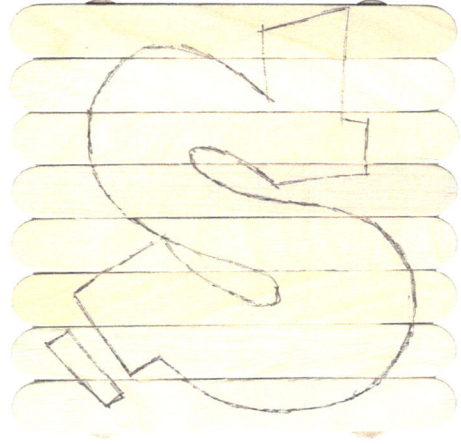

ERASE
THE
INSIDE
PENCIL
LINES

DARKEN
THE
OUTLINE

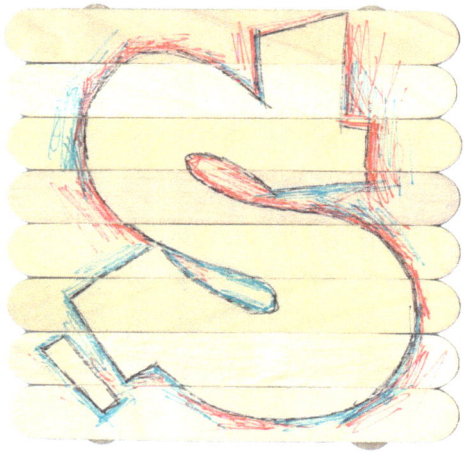

STEP 3. I added yellow and purple.

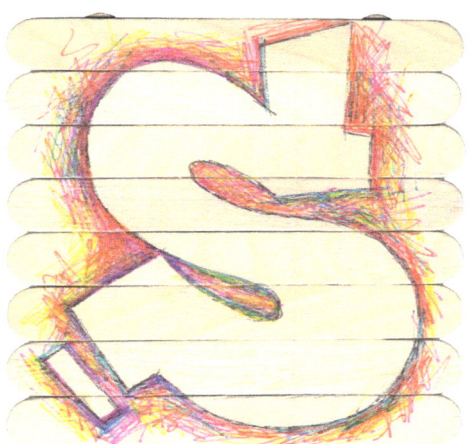

STEP 4. I added green and orange.

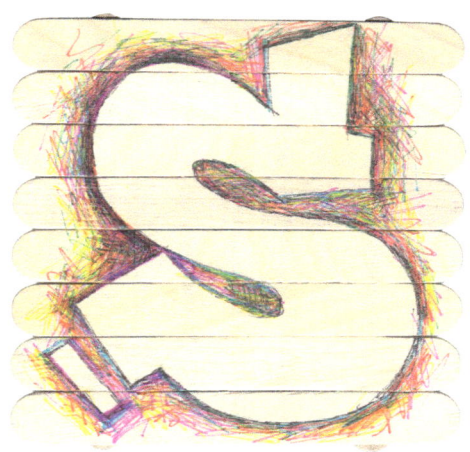

STEP 5. I added brown and dark blue.

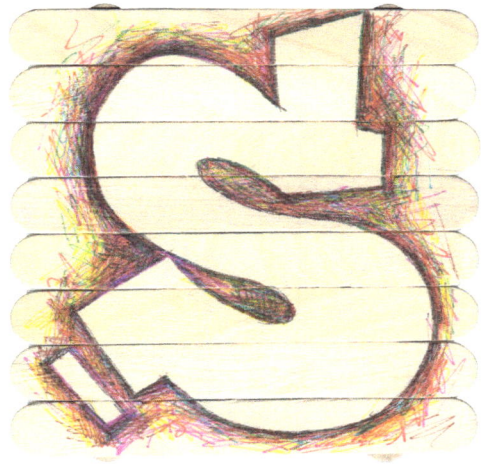

STEP 6. I went over the whole piece with black.

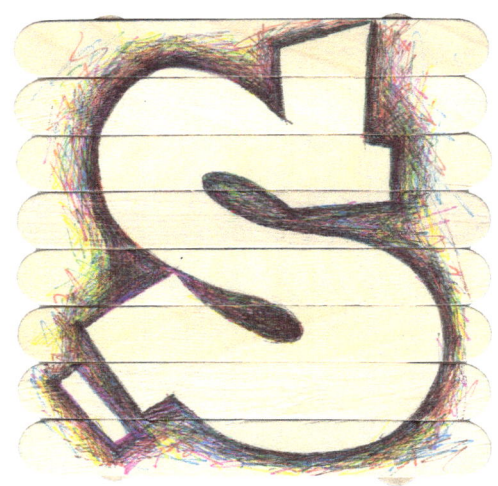

SCRIBBLE TECHNIQUE ON A BLACK BACKGROUND

You will need black paint and a white, light grey or light yellow colored pencil. I used all three.

STEP 1. Make a wood plaque and trace it onto a piece of paper. On the paper sketch out a Wildstyle letter.

STEP 2. Cut the paper letter out. You will use this cutout as a stencil. You can find this project on page 35 to see how it looks finished.

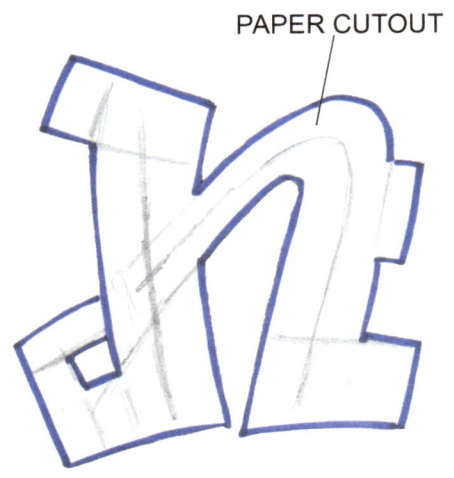

PAPER CUTOUT

STEP 3. Paint a wood plaque with a coat of watery black acrylic paint. Let it dry thoroughly.

STEP 4. Place the paper letter cutout onto the plaque and trace it with a white colored pencil.

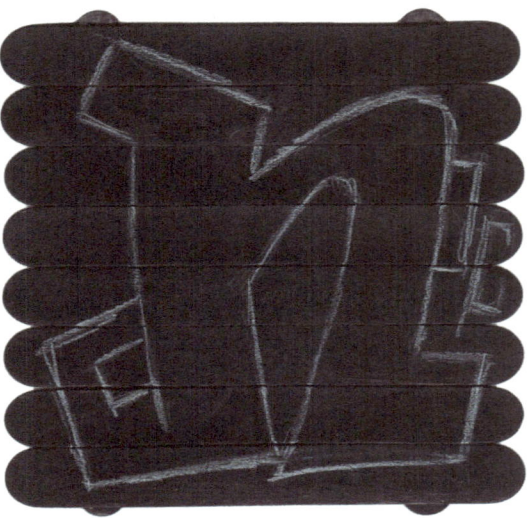

STEP 5. Scribble around the outside of the letter with a white pencil. You can also use a light grey or a light yellow pencil as well to add depth of color.

STEP 6. Build up the color until it's bright. Apply a coat of Varnish. When dry, glue rhinestones or sequins inside the letter for highlights.

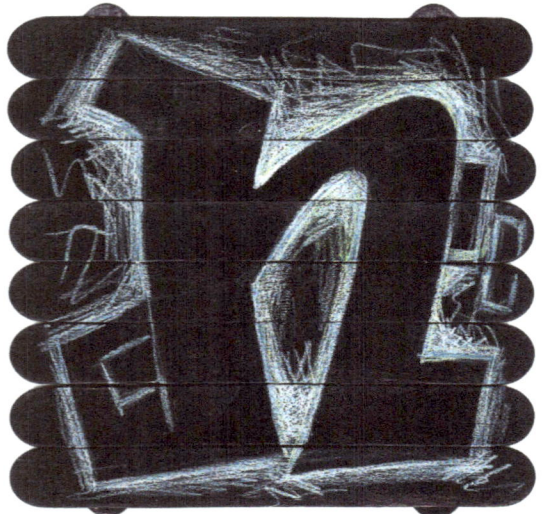

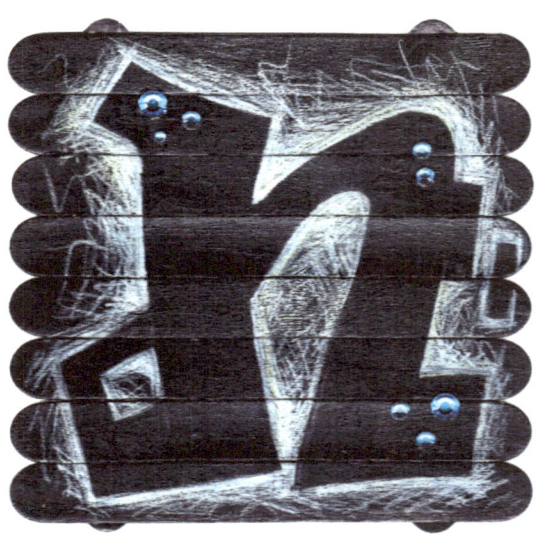

YOU CAN DECORATE WITH ACRYLIC PAINT, COLORED PENCILS, OR CRAYONS

You don't have to decorate your plaques with scribbles or magic markers. You can color your Wildstyle letters with acrylic paints or colored pencils. Popsicle sticks are really easy to draw and color on because they are made from real wood. They are water-resistant and can be rubbed with sandpaper to correct small errors.

Keep it simple and clean with acrylic paint. Paint with bright colors.

Add sequins, rhinestones or just plain paint dots for highlights.

1
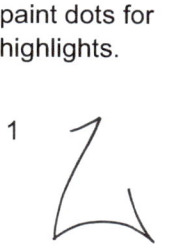

2
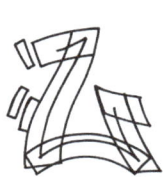

3
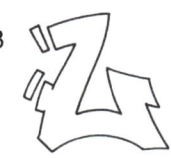

4
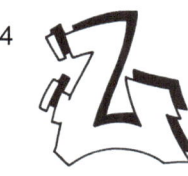

Combine colored pencils with acrylic paints and permanent magic markers. Experiment with all of the tools you have on hand and see what kind of amazing effects you can create.

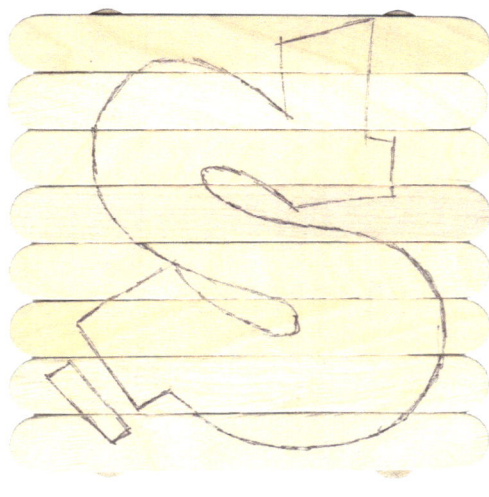

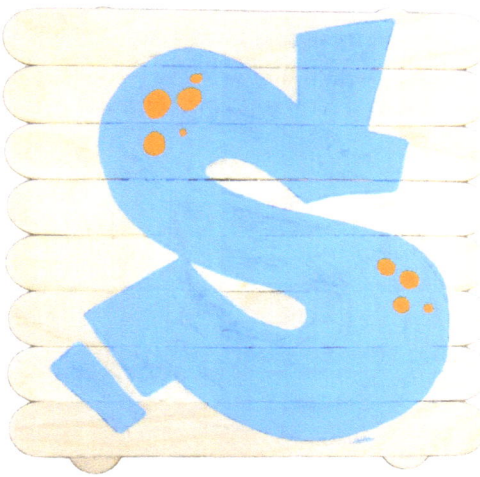

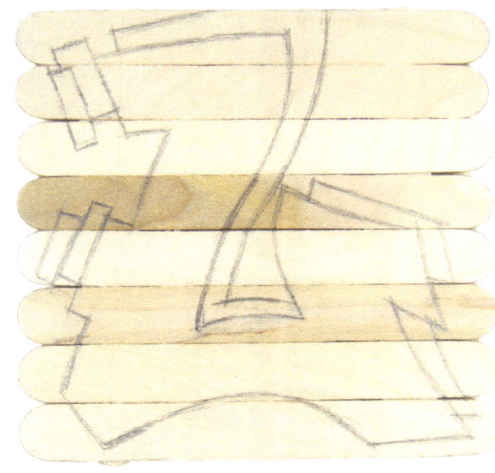

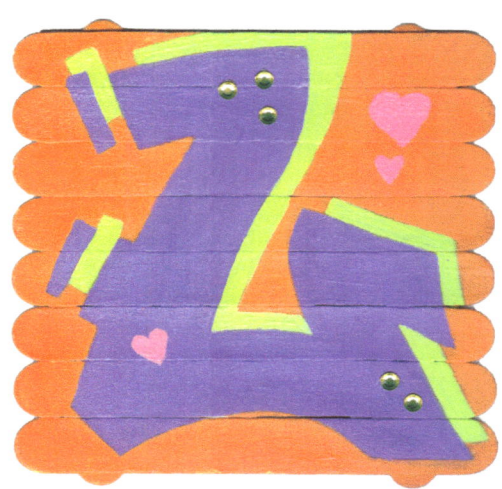

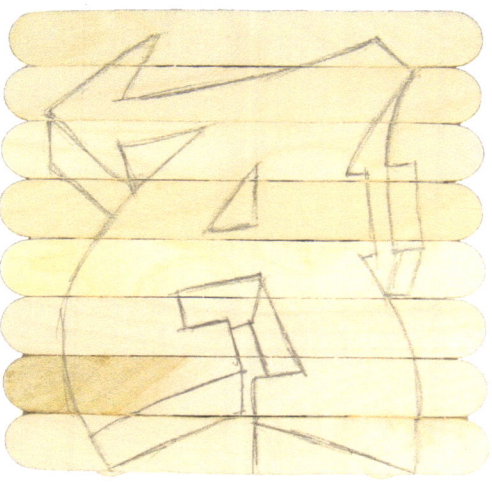

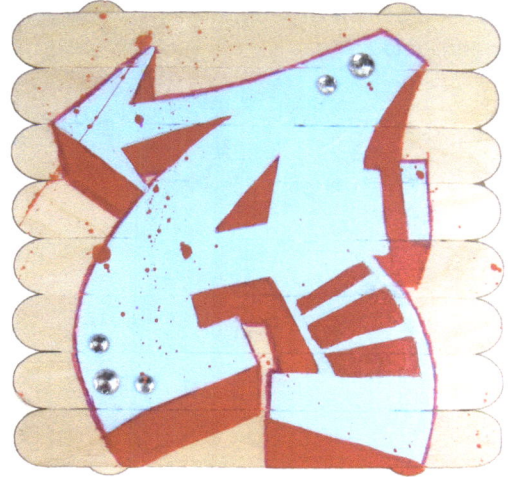

SCRIBBLE TECHNIQUE ON A COLORED BACKGROUND

You don't have to settle for plain wood projects. Try lots of different colors in different combinations to see what looks good. This technique uses acrylic paint and Ultra-Fine Point Sharpies, but you might like to try colored pencils over the paint instead.

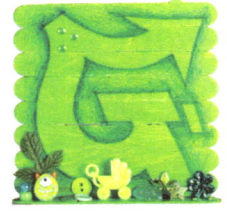
SEE PAGE 28

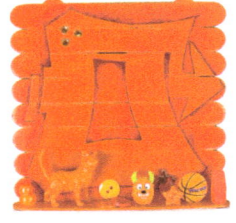
SEE PAGE 36

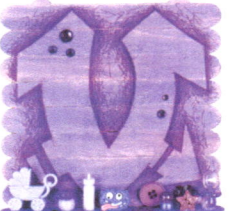
SEE PAGE 43

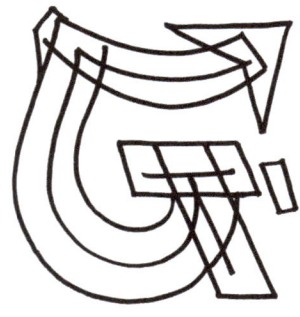
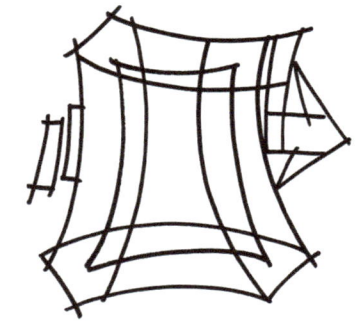
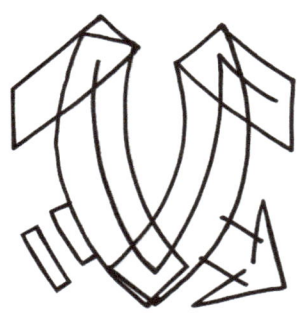

STEP 1. With a pencil draw tag letters G, O, and V on wood plaques. Draw bars around the strokes using The Plank Method on page 4. You'll find the break-downs for these letters on pages 28, 36, and 43.

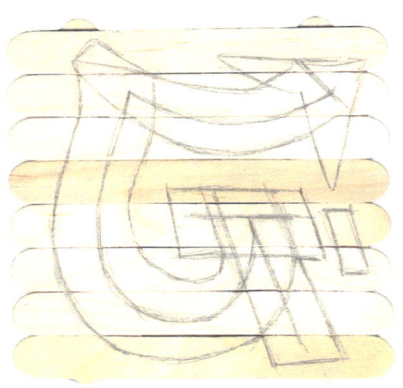
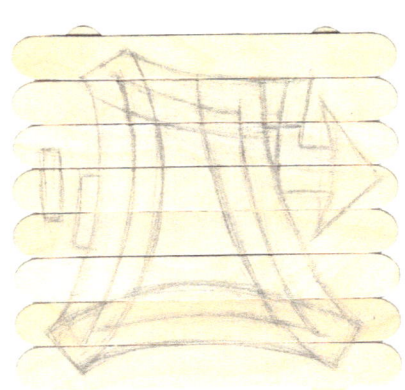
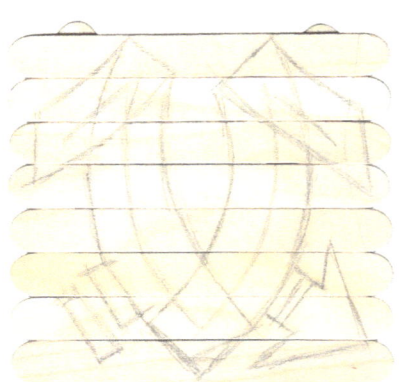

STEP 2. Draw around the outside edge with an Ultra-Fine Point Sharpie or a colored pencil. Erase the inside pencil lines. Make sure the outline is dark and the lines are clear. For the orange plaque, add red or brown.

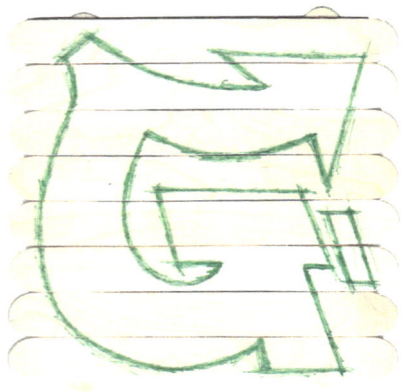
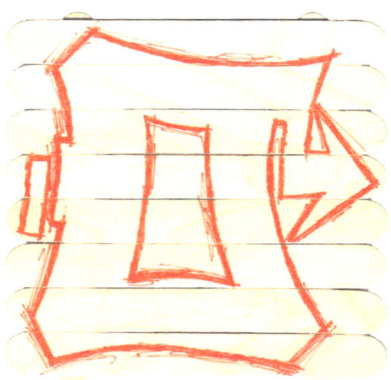
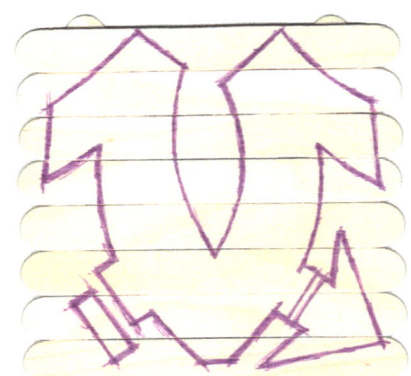

STEP 3. Paint the plaques with a coat of watery paint in the coordinating color as shown. The letter underneath should show through the paint. When the paint is dry rub the surface with a rough cloth such as a dish towel. This will seal the wood and make it easier to draw on top of as well as protect the felt tips of your markers.

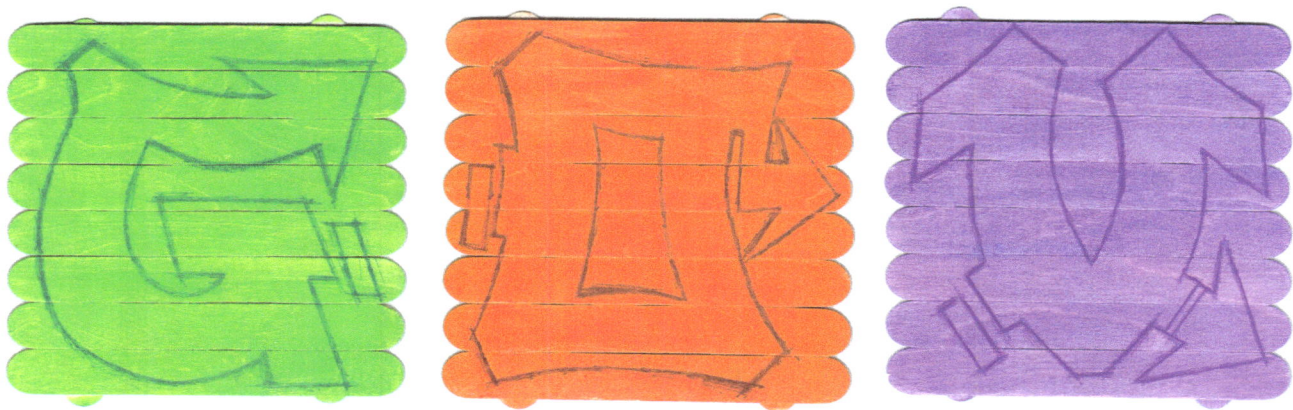

STEP 4. Now go over the outline with a Sharpie or a colored pencil. Scribble around the outside edge. On the orange plaque, you might want to use brown or red because orange will be too light to see.

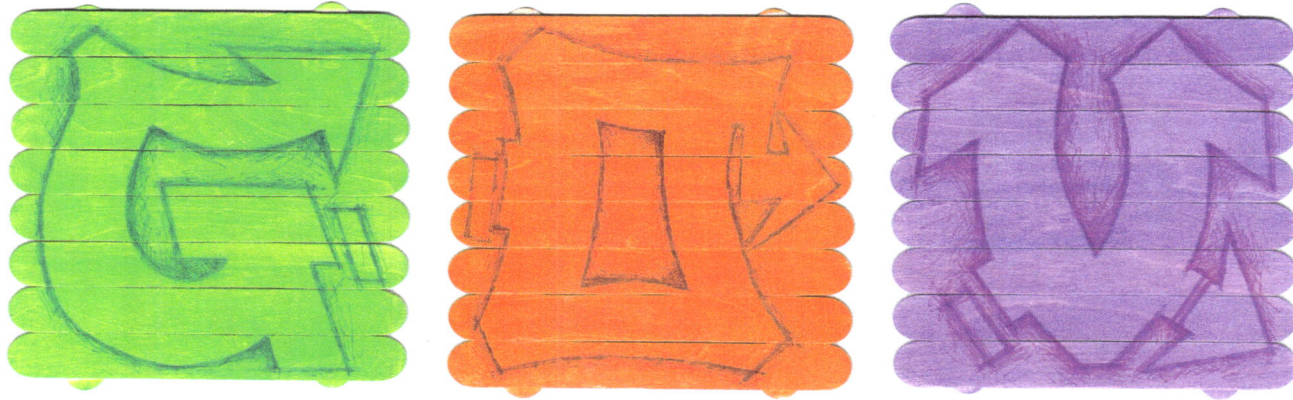

STEP 5. Press down firmly and make your letters really stand out. Continue to add color until your design looks finished to you. Then apply a coat of Varnish.

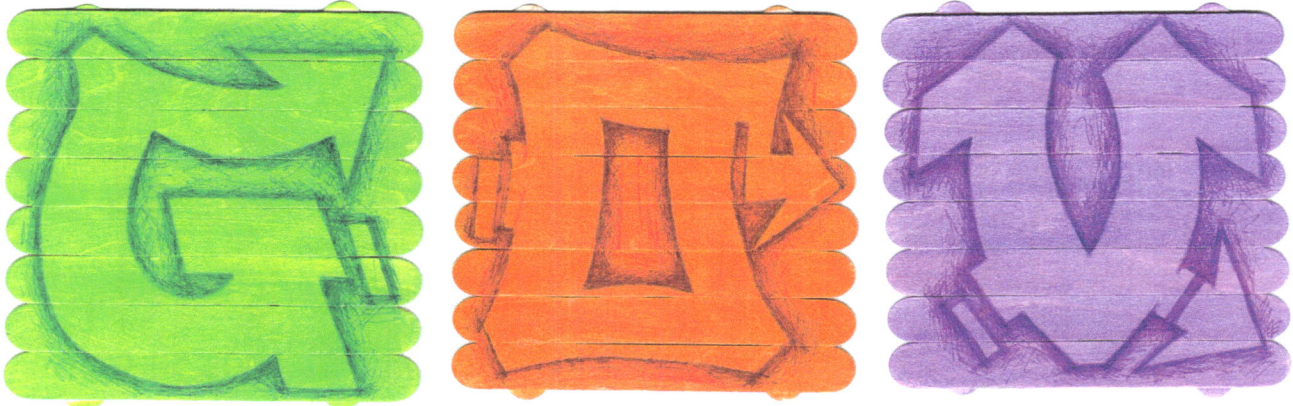

See the finished projects on pages 28, 36, and 43. They are spectacular. When the project is dry, add sequins, rhinestones, or use a glitter marker to create shiny highlights.

ATTACHING A SHELF

STEP 1. On the back of a plaque put a piece of blue tape or masking tape.

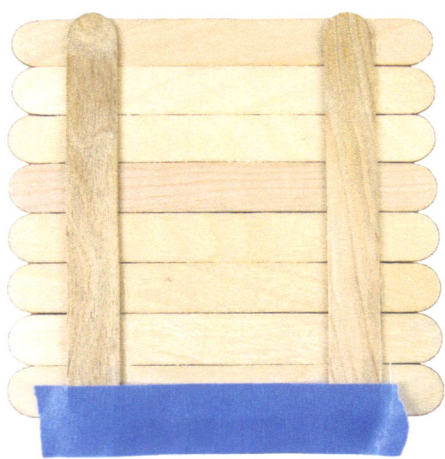

STEP 2. Put glue along the bottom edge. Extra thick tacky glue works best.

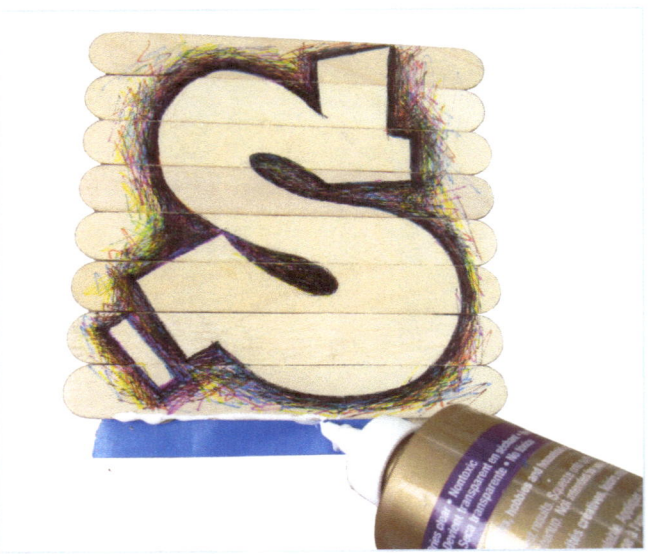

STEP 3. Press the popsicle stick shelf (from page 14) into the glue. Hold it in place for a few seconds.

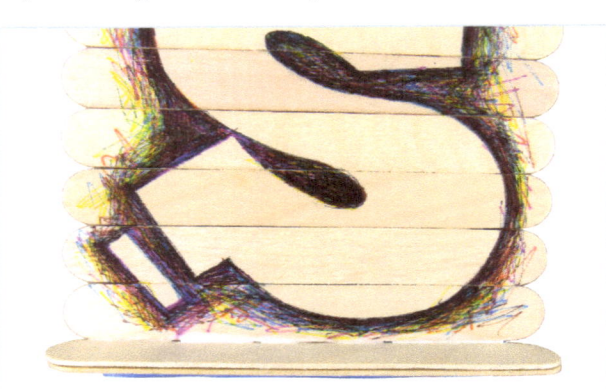

STEP 4. Fold the tape up under the bottom to hold the shelf in place. You may have to readjust it a bit.

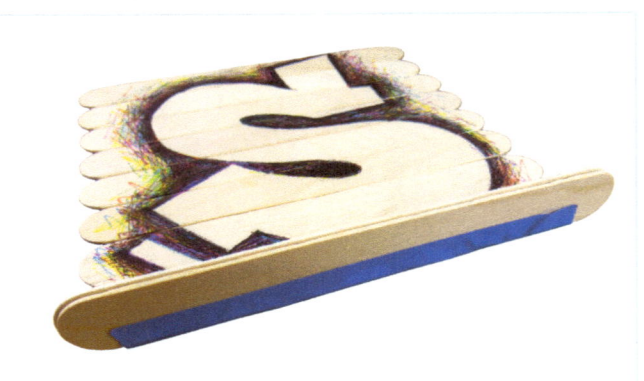

STEP 5. Coat the joint on the front of the shelf and the plaque with Mod Podge or Varnish. This will make your project much stronger and prevent the shelf from sagging. Let it dry thoroughly before gluing on ornaments.

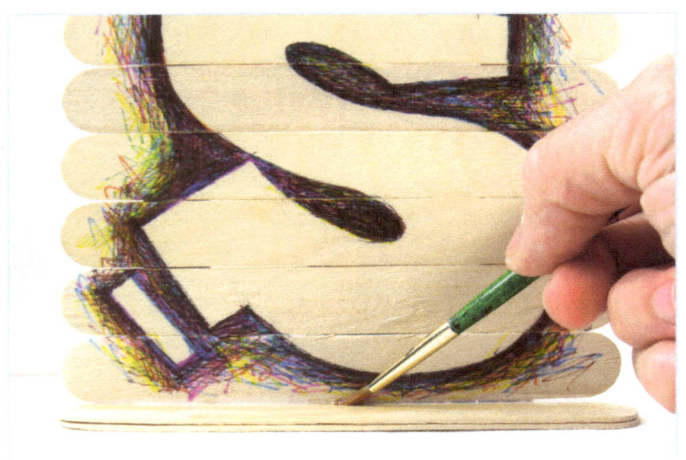

STEP 6. Stand the project up and lean the back against a bottle or some other object to help it dry in the correct position. Allow the glue and Mod Podge or Varnish to set for a few hours.

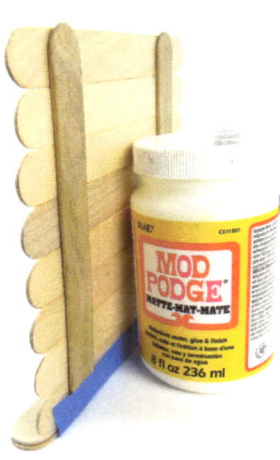

HANGING OR STANDING THE PLAQUE FOR DISPLAY

ATTACHING A BACK STAND

STEP 1. Glue two sticks together.
STEP 2. Glue on a single stick at a right angle. Let it dry.
STEP 3. Coat the joint with Mod Podge or Varnish.
STEP 4. Glue stand to the back of the project.

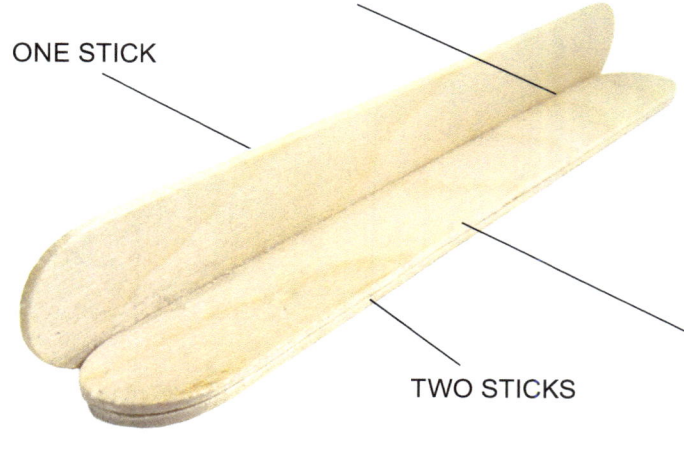

COAT WITH MOD PODGE OR VARNISH

ONE STICK

TWO STICKS

ATTACHING A STRING

STEP 1. Spread a line of glue in the crevice on the outside edge of the back sticks. Do both sides.

STEP 2. Press a string into the glue. Let the glue dry thoroughly before hanging.

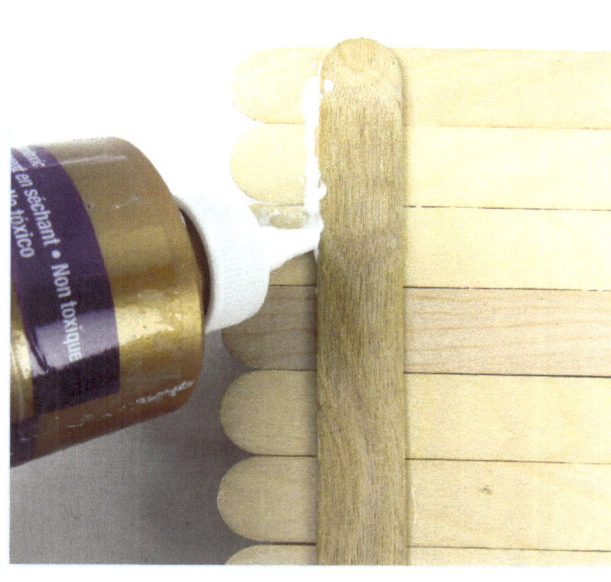

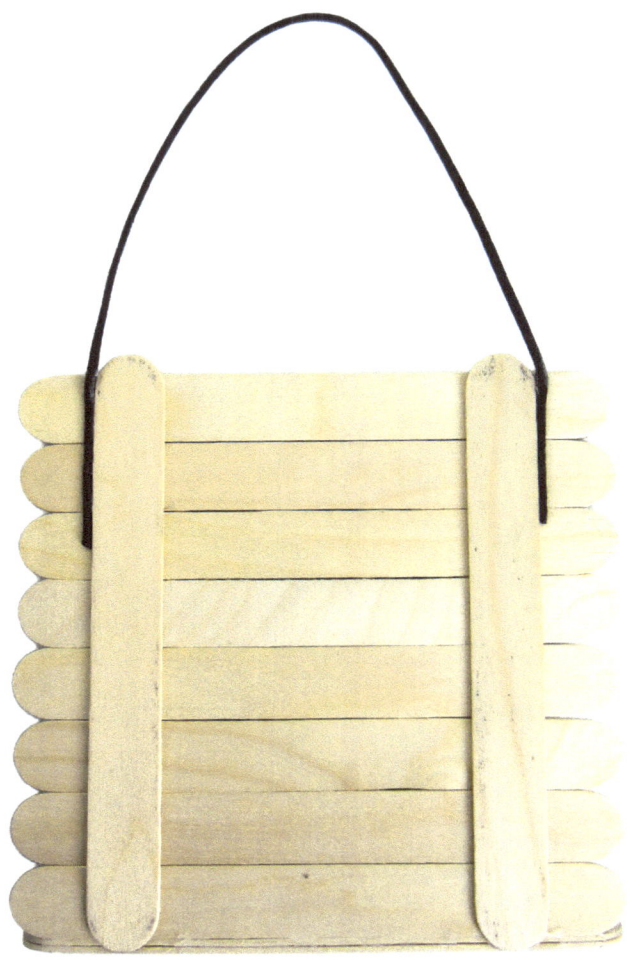

A is for Apple

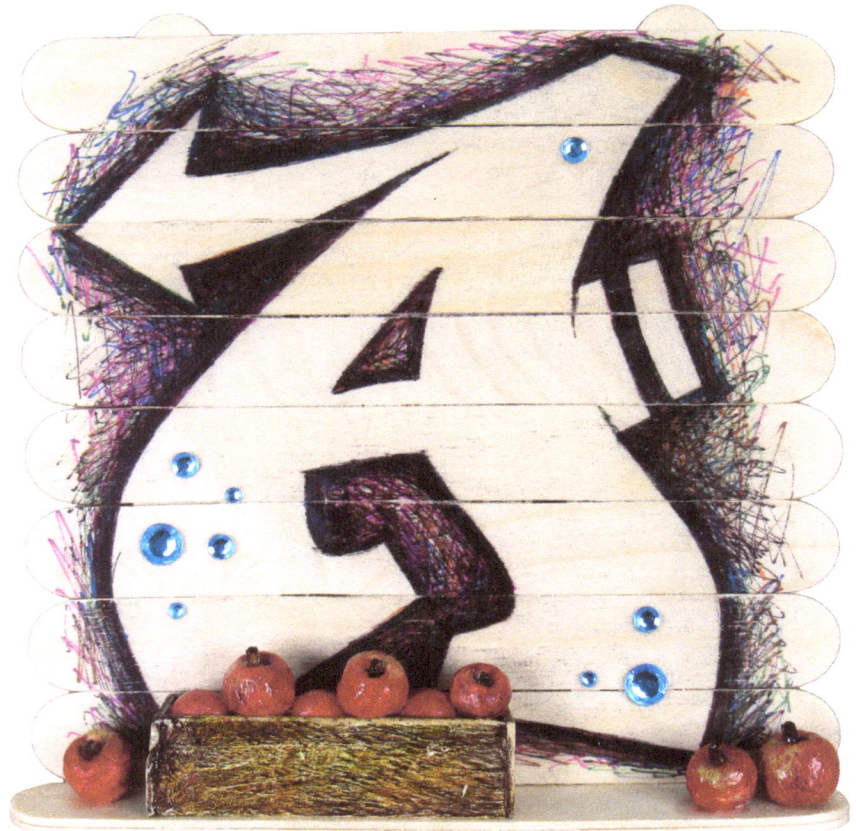

The apples are made with air-dry clay. The crate is made with popsicle sticks. See page 50.

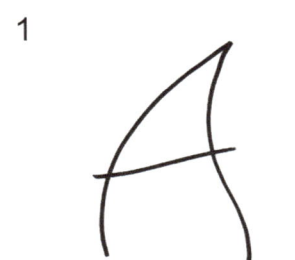

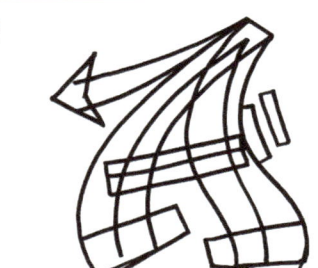

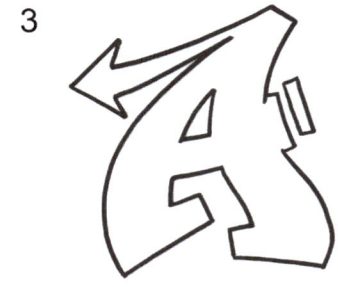

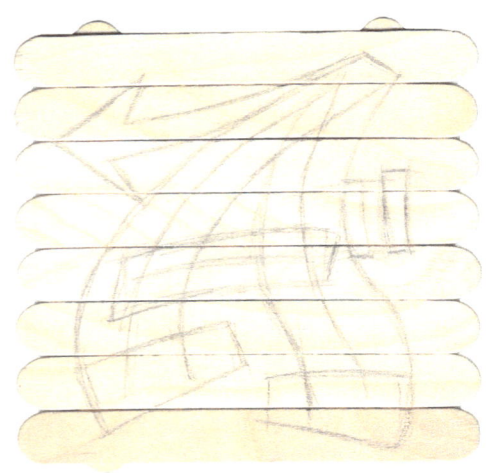

STEP 1. Make a wood plaque (see page 14).

STEP 2. With a pencil draw a Wildstyle letter onto the plaque. Use the Plank Method (see page 4) and the diagram above as a guide.

STEP 3. Draw a dark outline around the outside edges of the letter with an Ultra-Fine Point Sharpie or a colored pencil.

STEP 4. Erase the pencil lines with a pink eraser. Rub vigorously.

STEP 5. Draw scribbles all around the outside of the letter (see page 15), or color in with paint, markers, colored pencils or crayons. Finish off with a coat of Varnish if desired.

STEP 6. Glue on rhinestones or sequins to create highlights.

STEP 7. Glue on a popsicle stick shelf (see page 20). Let dry.

STEP 8. Assemble the small ornaments you need (see page 48).

STEP 9. Glue them on and coat with Varnish or Mod Podge.

STEP 10. Attach a hanger or a back stand to display (see page 21).

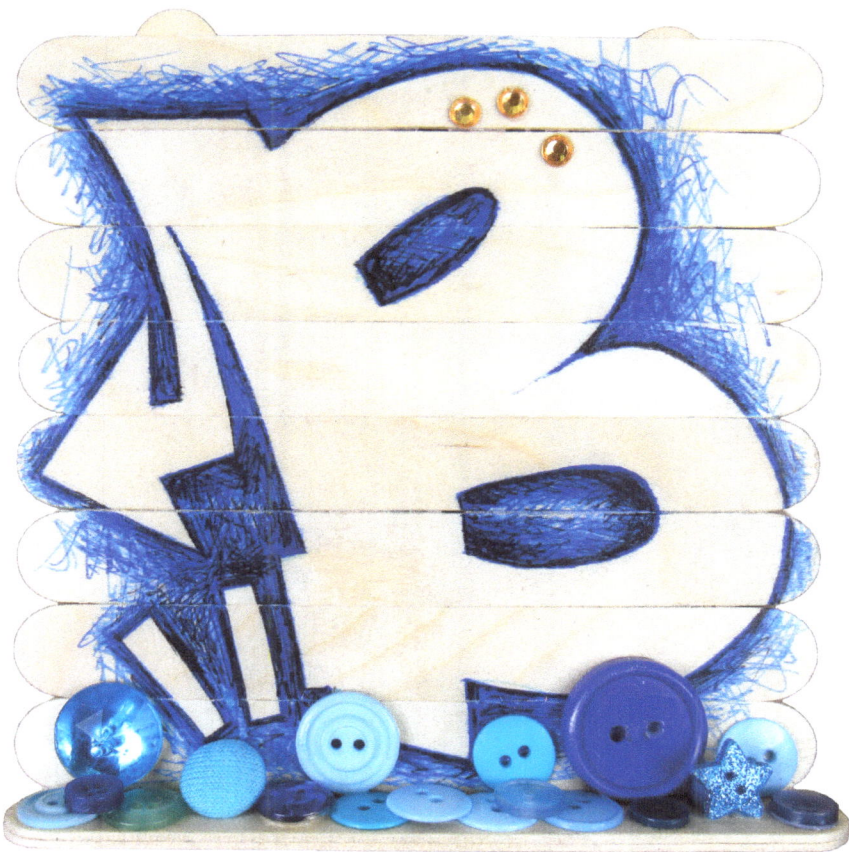

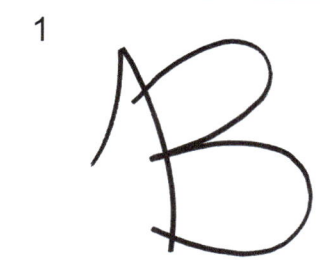

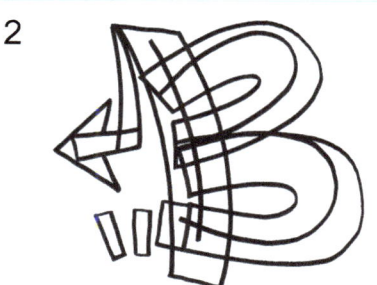

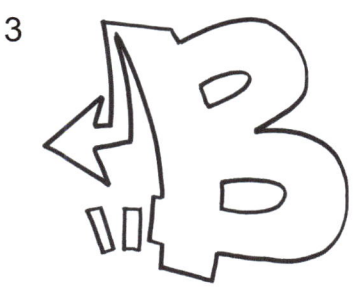

STEP 1. Make a wood plaque (see page 14).

STEP 2. With a pencil draw a Wildstyle letter onto the plaque. Use the Plank Method (see page 4) and the diagram above as a guide.

STEP 3. Draw a dark outline around the outside edges of the letter with an Ultra-Fine Point Sharpie or a colored pencil.

STEP 4. Erase the pencil lines with a pink eraser. Rub vigorously.

STEP 5. Draw scribbles all around the outside of the letter (see page 15), or color in with paint, markers, colored pencils or crayons. Finish off with a coat of Varnish if desired.

STEP 6. Glue on rhinestones or sequins to create highlights.

STEP 7. Glue on a popsicle stick shelf (see page 20). Let dry.

STEP 8. Assemble the small ornaments you need (see page 48).

STEP 9. Glue them on and coat with Varnish or Mod Podge.

STEP 10. Attach a hanger or a back stand to display (see page 21).

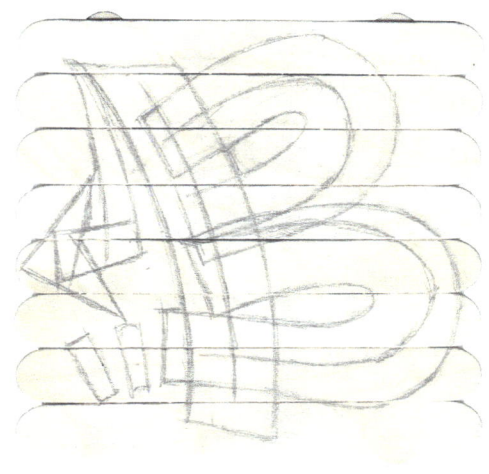

C is for Conch Shells (and Coral)

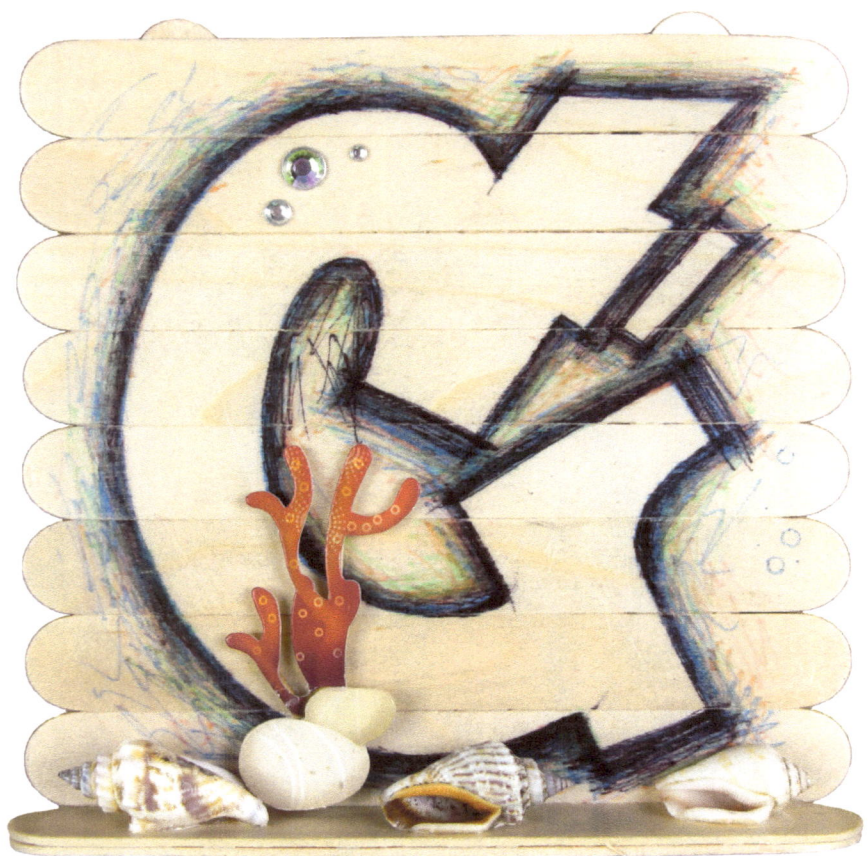

The shells are real conch shells from the dollar store. The coral is a paper sticker.

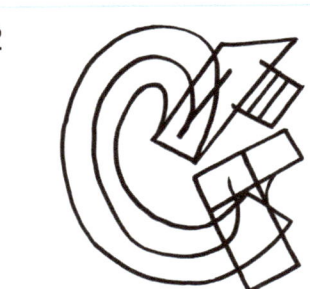

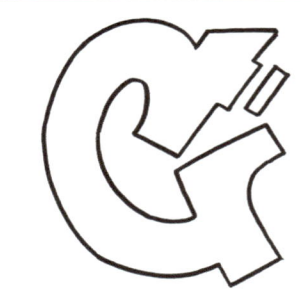

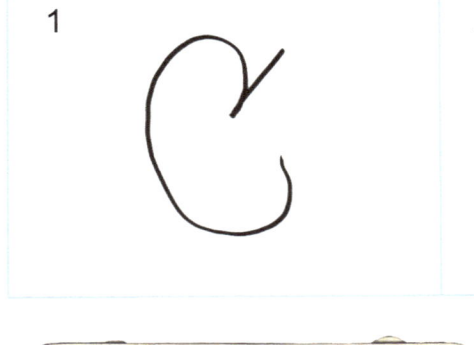

STEP 1. Make a wood plaque (see page 14).

STEP 2. With a pencil draw a Wildstyle letter onto the plaque. Use the Plank Method (see page 4) and the diagram above as a guide.

STEP 3. Draw a dark outline around the outside edges of the letter with an Ultra-Fine Point Sharpie or a colored pencil.

STEP 4. Erase the pencil lines with a pink eraser. Rub vigorously.

STEP 5. Draw scribbles all around the outside of the letter (see page 15), or color in with paint, markers, colored pencils or crayons. Finish off with a coat of Varnish if desired.

STEP 6. Glue on rhinestones or sequins to create highlights.

STEP 7. Glue on a popsicle stick shelf (see page 20). Let dry.

STEP 8. Assemble the small ornaments you need (see page 48).

STEP 9. Glue them on and coat with Varnish or Mod Podge.

STEP 10. Attach a hanger or a back stand to display (see page 21).

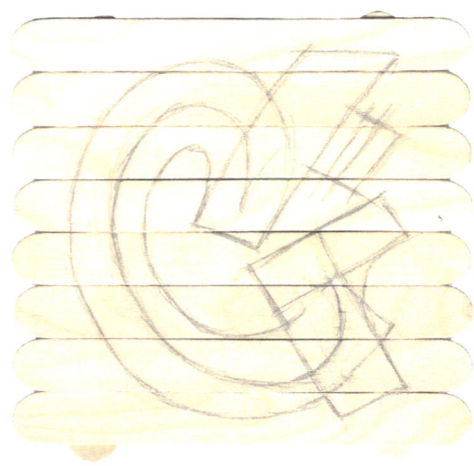

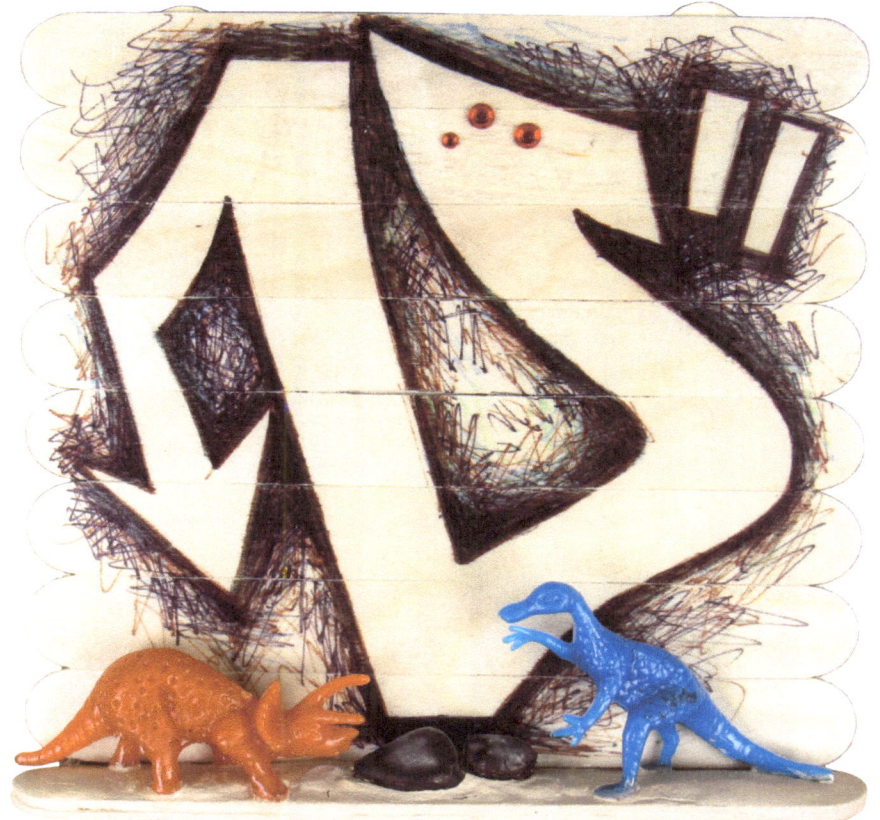

1

2

3

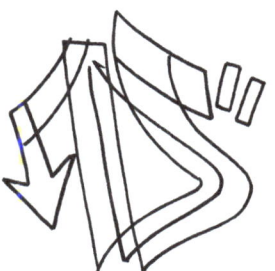

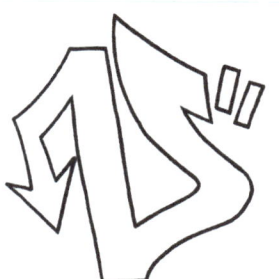

STEP 1. Make a wood plaque (see page 14).
STEP 2. With a pencil draw a Wildstyle letter onto the plaque. Use the Plank Method (see page 4) and the diagram above as a guide.
STEP 3. Draw a dark outline around the outside edges of the letter with an Ultra-Fine Point Sharpie or a colored pencil.
STEP 4. Erase the pencil lines with a pink eraser. Rub vigorously.
STEP 5. Draw scribbles all around the outside of the letter (see page 15), or color in with paint, markers, colored pencils or crayons. Finish off with a coat of Varnish if desired.
STEP 6. Glue on rhinestones or sequins to create highlights.
STEP 7. Glue on a popsicle stick shelf (see page 20). Let dry.
STEP 8. Assemble the small ornaments you need (see page 48).
STEP 9. Glue them on and coat with Varnish or Mod Podge.
STEP 10. Attach a hanger or a back stand to display (see page 21).

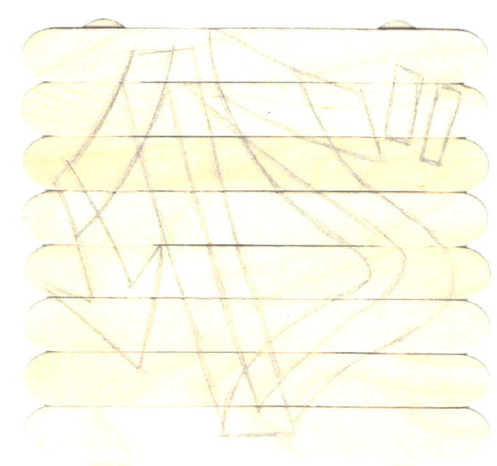

E is for Erasers

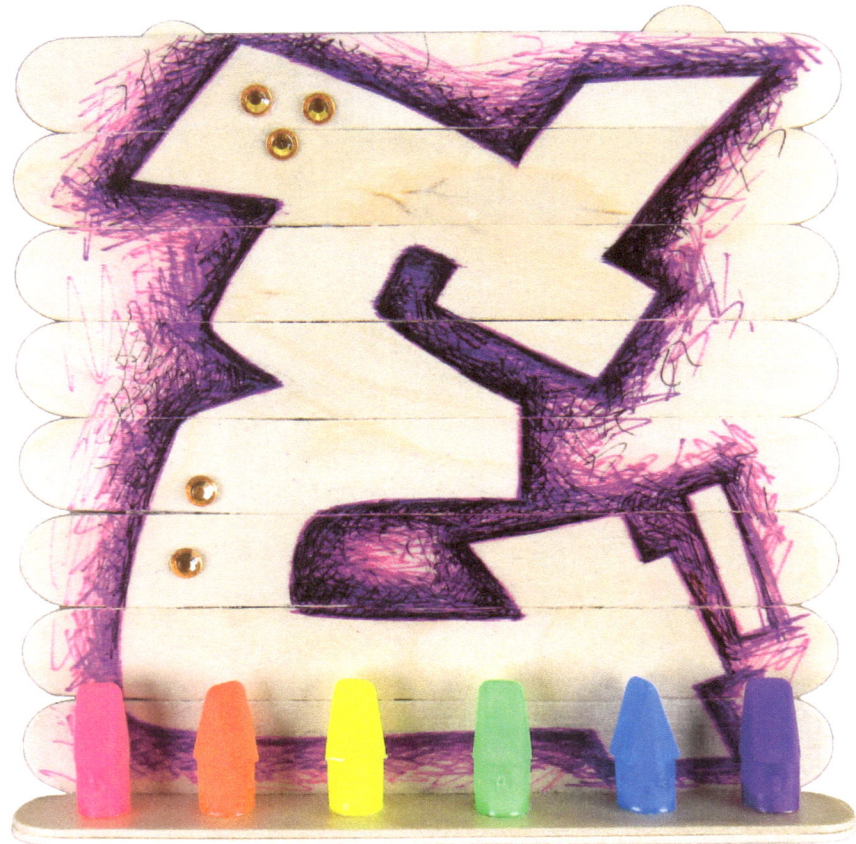

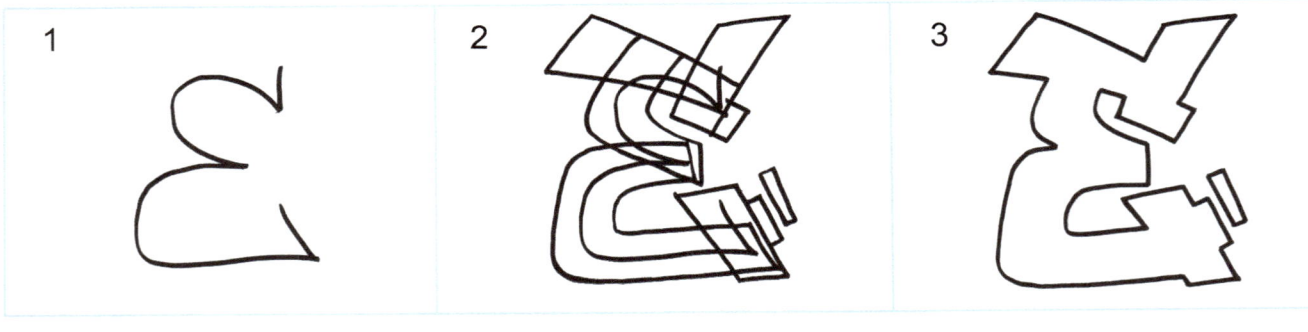

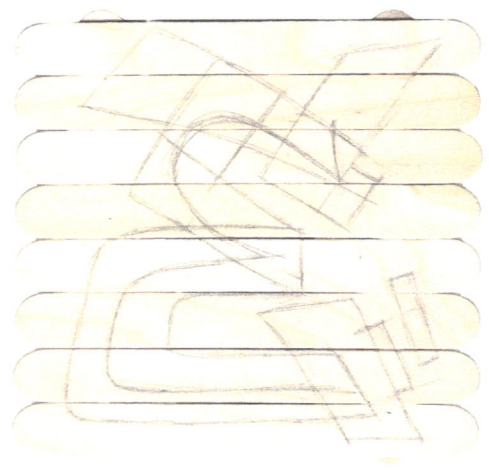

STEP 1. Make a wood plaque (see page 14).

STEP 2. With a pencil draw a Wildstyle letter onto the plaque. Use the Plank Method (see page 4) and the diagram above as a guide.

STEP 3. Draw a dark outline around the outside edges of the letter with an Ultra-Fine Point Sharpie or a colored pencil.

STEP 4. Erase the pencil lines with a pink eraser. Rub vigorously.

STEP 5. Draw scribbles all around the outside of the letter (see page 15), or color in with paint, markers, colored pencils or crayons. Finish off with a coat of Varnish if desired.

STEP 6. Glue on rhinestones or sequins to create highlights.

STEP 7. Glue on a popsicle stick shelf (see page 20). Let dry.

STEP 8. Assemble the small ornaments you need (see page 48).

STEP 9. Glue them on and coat with Varnish or Mod Podge.

STEP 10. Attach a hanger or a back stand to display (see page 21).

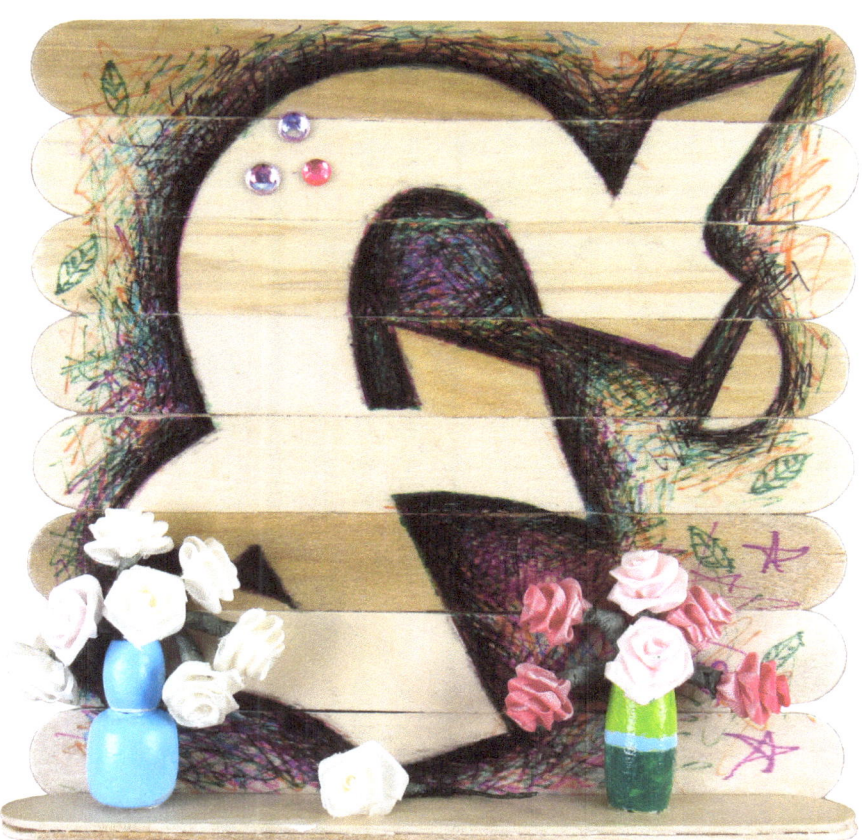

To make these
flower vases,
see page 51.

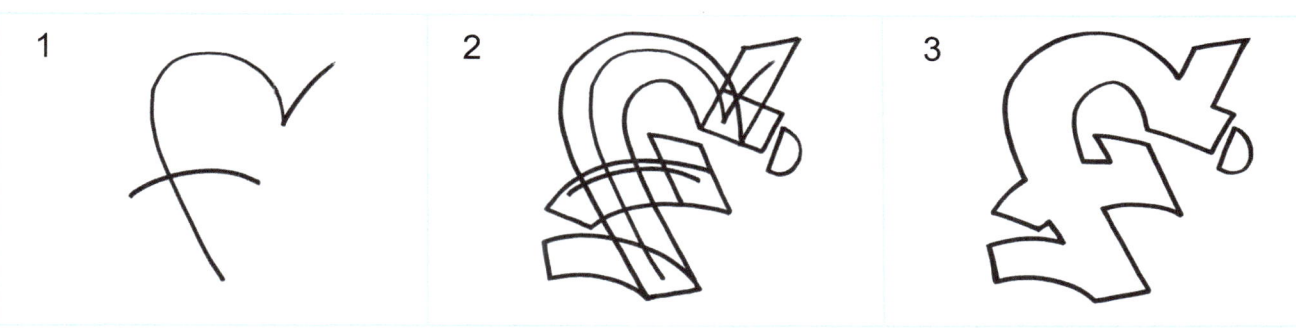

1   2   3

STEP 1. Make a wood plaque (see page 14).
STEP 2. With a pencil draw a Wildstyle letter onto the plaque. Use the lowercase f in the diagram or the uppercase F on page 11.
STEP 3. Draw a dark outline around the outside edges of the letter with an Ultra-Fine Point Sharpie or a colored pencil.
STEP 4. Erase the pencil lines with a pink eraser. Rub vigorously.
STEP 5. Draw scribbles all around the outside of the letter (see page 15), or color in with paint, markers, colored pencils or crayons. Finish off with a coat of Varnish if desired.
STEP 6. Glue on rhinestones or sequins to create highlights.
STEP 7. Glue on a popsicle stick shelf (see page 20). Let dry.
STEP 8. Assemble the small ornaments you need (see page 48).
STEP 9. Glue them on and coat with Varnish or Mod Podge.
STEP 10. Attach a hanger or a back stand to display (see page 21).

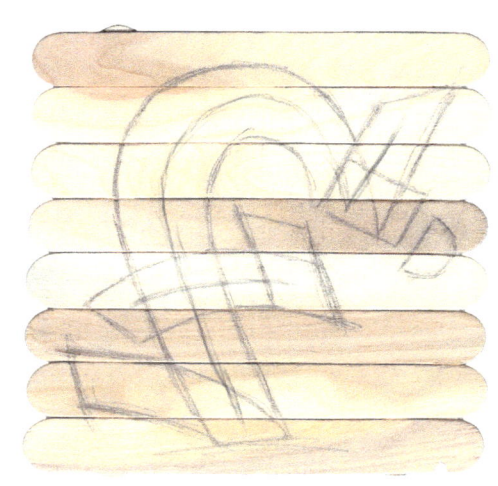

G is for Green

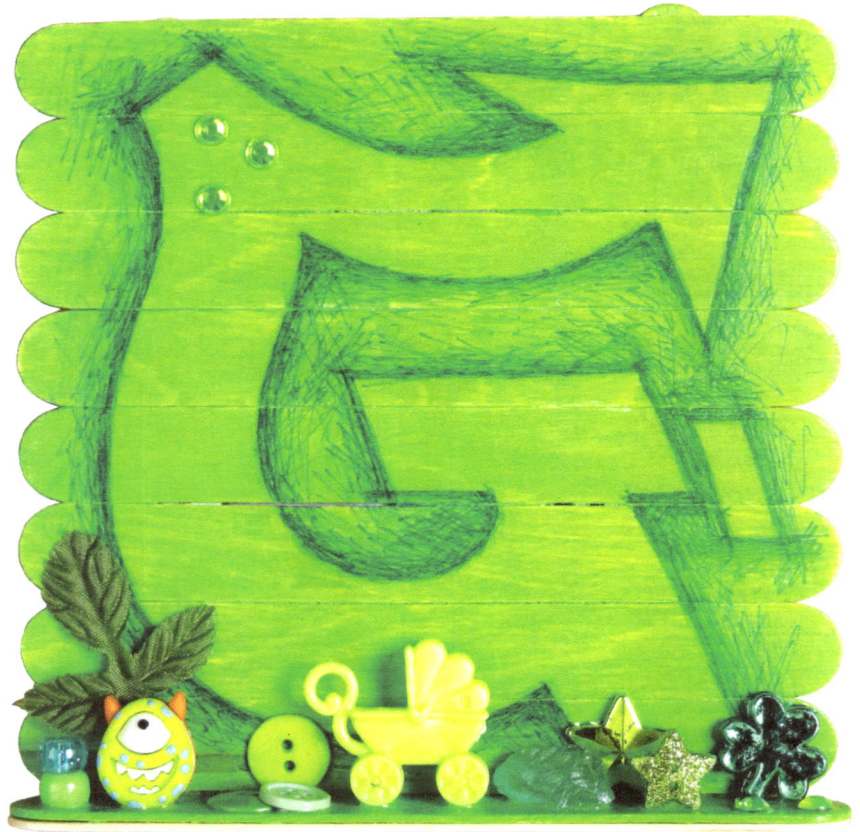

I used a pre-made monster button but you can make your own monster with the instructions on page 51.

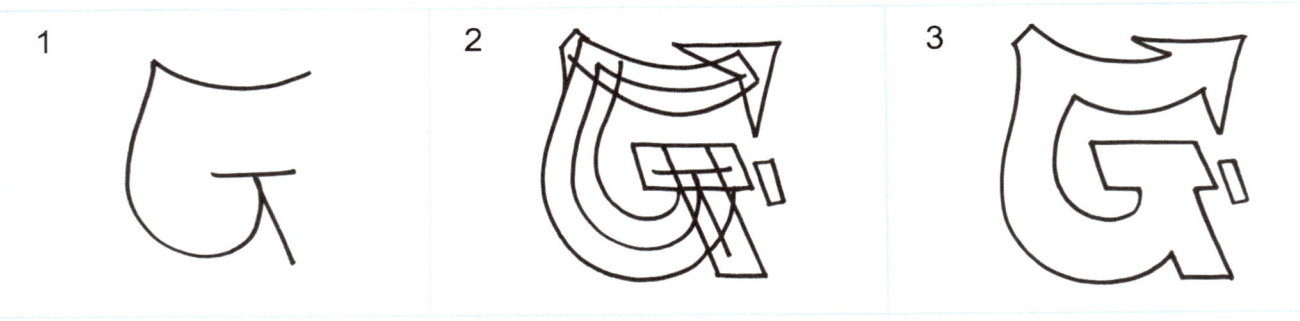

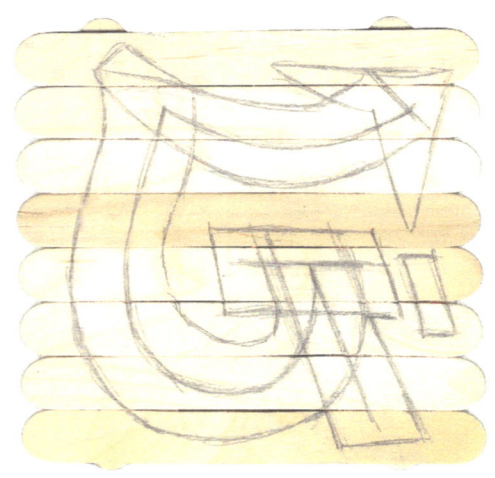

STEP 1. Make a wood plaque (see page 14).
STEP 2. With a pencil draw a Wildstyle letter onto the plaque. Use the Plank Method (see page 4) and the diagram above as a guide.
STEP 3. Draw a dark outline around the outside edges of the letter with an Ultra-Fine Point Sharpie or a colored pencil.
STEP 4. Erase the pencil lines with a pink eraser. Rub vigorously.
STEP 5. You can paint this plaque following the instructions on pages 18-19. Or decorate it any other way you like.
STEP 6. Glue on rhinestones or sequins to create highlights.
STEP 7. Glue on a popsicle stick shelf (see page 20). Let dry.
STEP 8. Assemble the small ornaments you need (see page 48).
STEP 9. Glue them on and coat with Varnish or Mod Podge.
STEP 10. Attach a hanger or a back stand to display (see page 21).

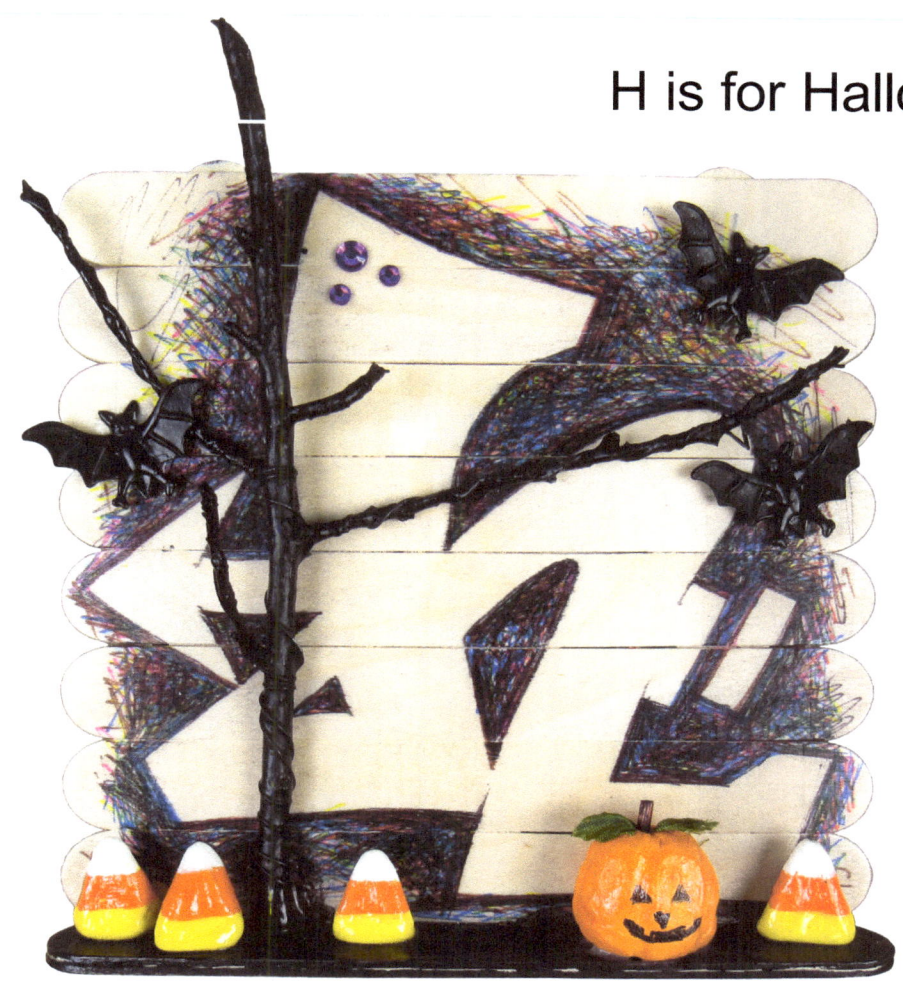

The bats are plastic rings from a dollar store with the ring part snipped off. To make the rest of these Halloween decorations, see page 52.

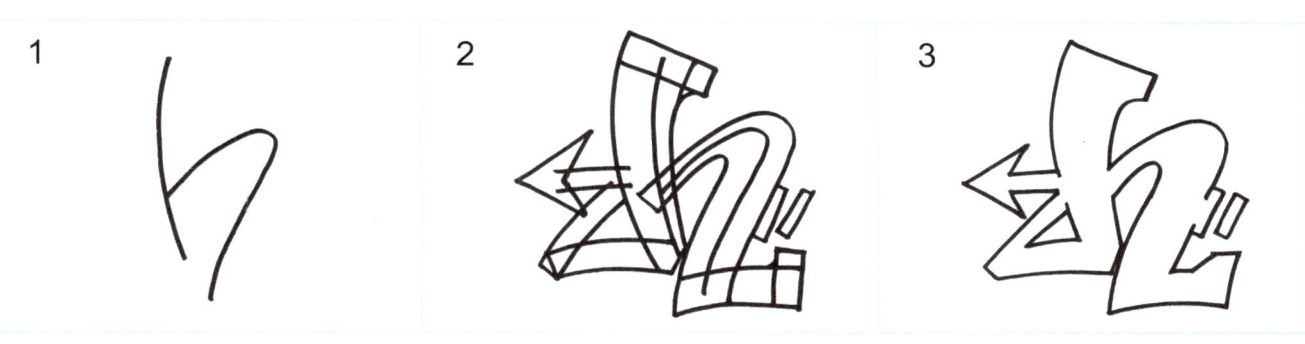

1

2

3

STEP 1. Make a wood plaque (see page 14).
STEP 2. With a pencil draw a Wildstyle letter onto the plaque. Use the lowercase h in the diagram or the uppercase H on page 11.
STEP 3. Draw a dark outline around the outside edges of the letter with an Ultra-Fine Point Sharpie or a colored pencil.
STEP 4. Erase the pencil lines with a pink eraser. Rub vigorously.
STEP 5. Draw scribbles all around the outside of the letter (see page 15), or color in with paint, markers, colored pencils or crayons. Finish off with a coat of Varnish if desired.
STEP 6. Glue on rhinestones or sequins to create highlights.
STEP 7. Glue on a popsicle stick shelf (see page 20). Let dry.
STEP 8. Assemble the small ornaments you need (see page 48).
STEP 9. Glue them on and coat with Varnish or Mod Podge.
STEP 10. Attach a hanger or a back stand to display (see page 21).

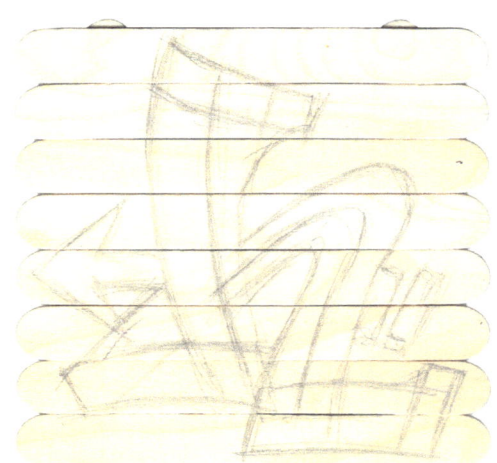

I is for Insects

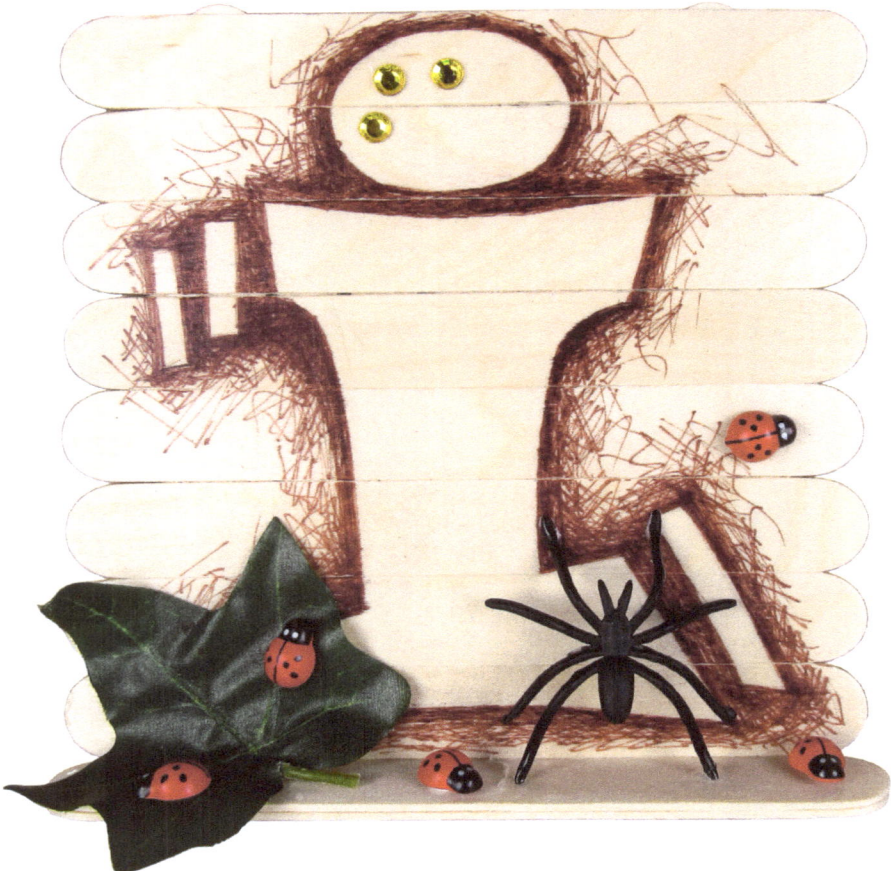

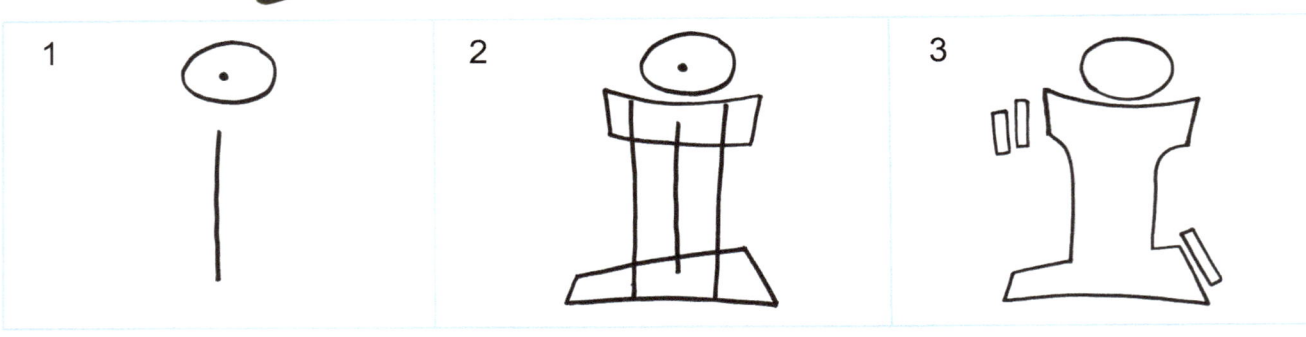

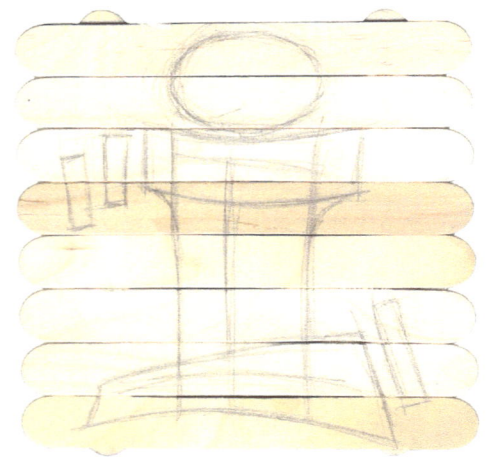

STEP 1. Make a wood plaque (see page 14).

STEP 2. With a pencil draw a Wildstyle letter onto the plaque. Use the lowercase i in the diagram or the uppercase I on page 11.

STEP 3. Draw a dark outline around the outside edges of the letter with an Ultra-Fine Point Sharpie or a colored pencil.

STEP 4. Erase the pencil lines with a pink eraser. Rub vigorously.

STEP 5. Draw scribbles all around the outside of the letter (see page 15), or color in with paint, markers, colored pencils or crayons. Finish off with a coat of Varnish if desired.

STEP 6. Glue on rhinestones or sequins to create highlights.

STEP 7. Glue on a popsicle stick shelf (see page 20). Let dry.

STEP 8. Assemble the small ornaments you need (see page 48).

STEP 9. Glue them on and coat with Varnish or Mod Podge.

STEP 10. Attach a hanger or a back stand to display (see page 21).

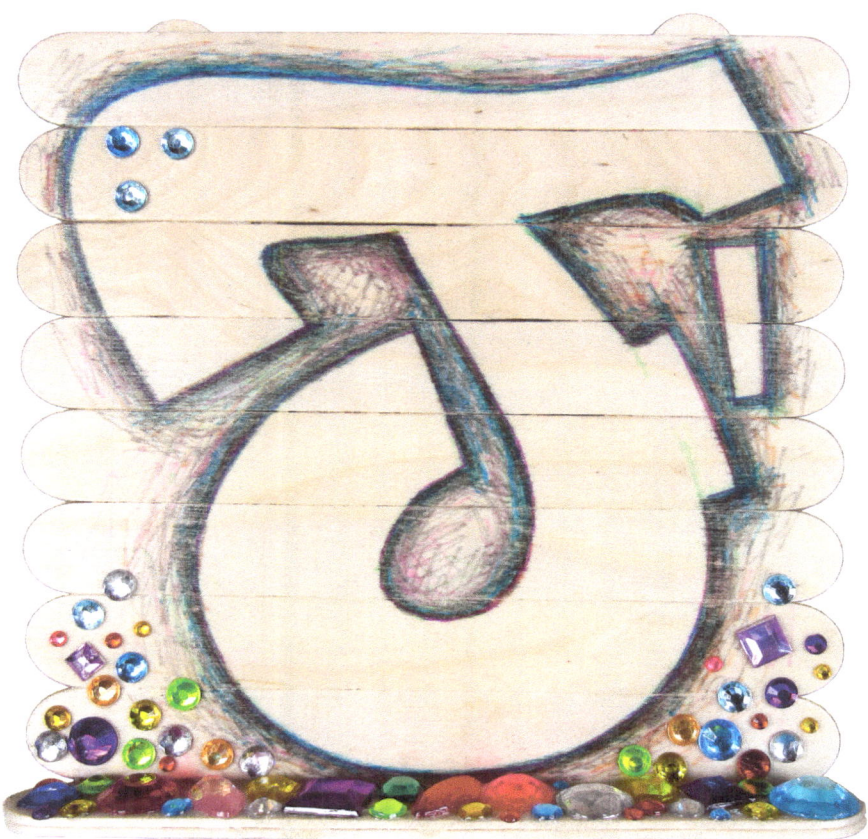

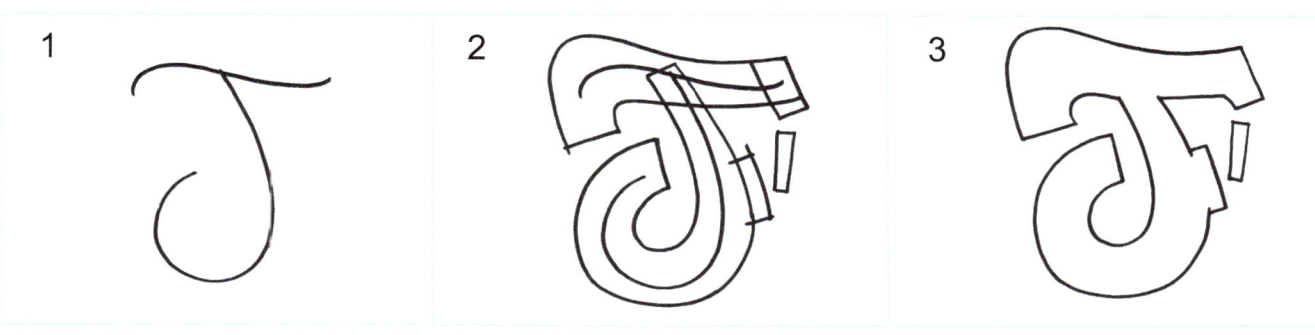

STEP 1. Make a wood plaque (see page 14).

STEP 2. With a pencil draw a Wildstyle letter onto the plaque. Use the Plank Method (see page 4) and the diagram above as a guide.

STEP 3. Draw a dark outline around the outside edges of the letter with an Ultra-Fine Point Sharpie or a colored pencil.

STEP 4. Erase the pencil lines with a pink eraser. Rub vigorously.

STEP 5. Draw scribbles all around the outside of the letter (see page 15), or color in with paint, markers, colored pencils or crayons. Finish off with a coat of Varnish if desired.

STEP 6. Glue on rhinestones or sequins to create highlights.

STEP 7. Glue on a popsicle stick shelf (see page 20). Let dry.

STEP 8. Assemble the small ornaments you need (see page 48).

STEP 9. Glue them on and coat with Varnish or Mod Podge.

STEP 10. Attach a hanger or a back stand to display (see page 21).

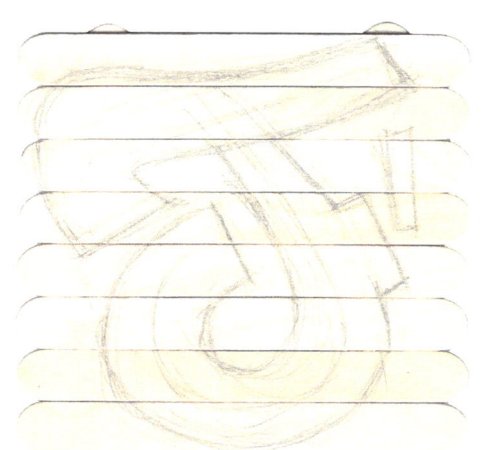

K is for Keyboard

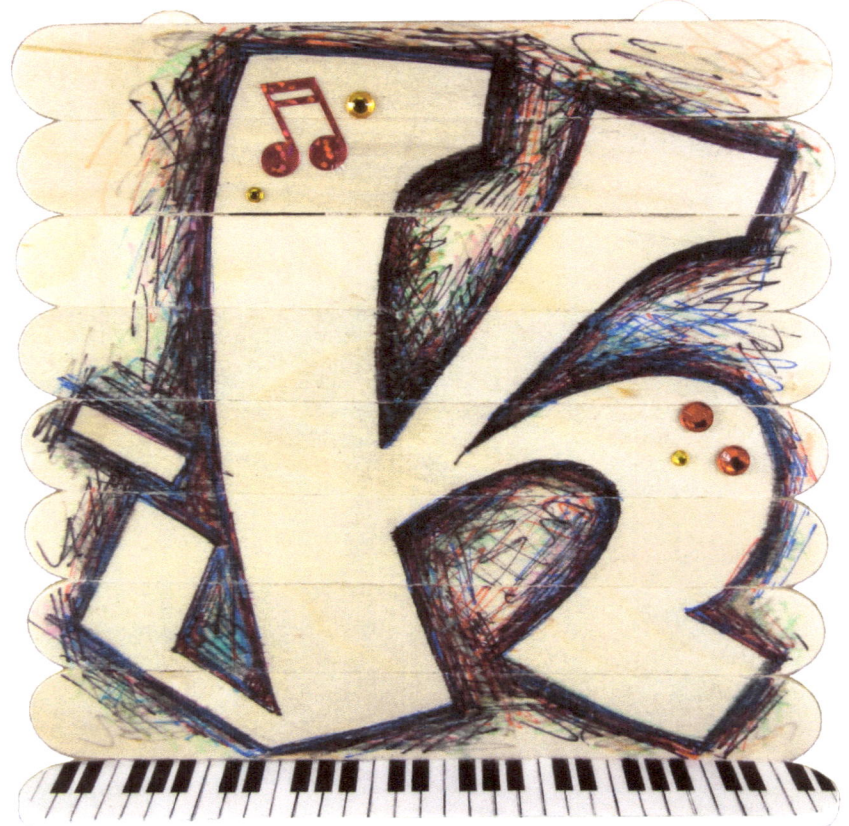

To make this Keyboard, see page 54.

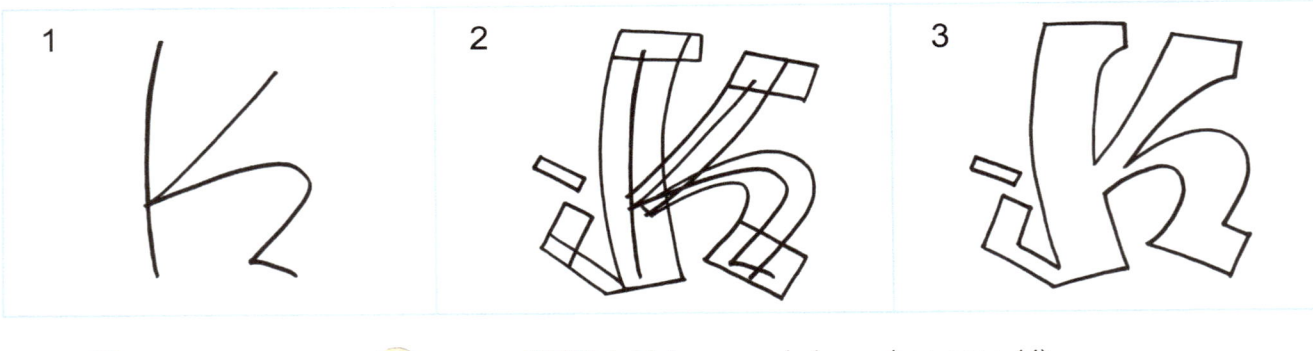

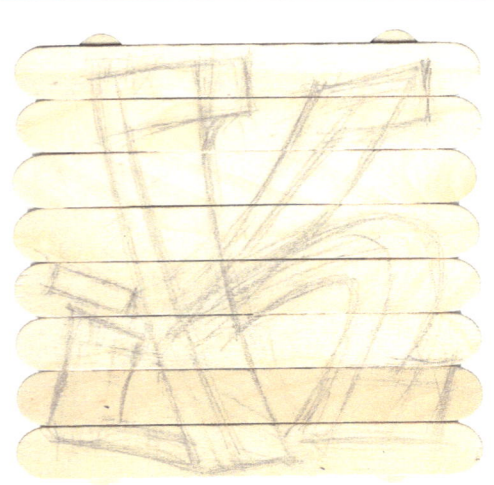

STEP 1. Make a wood plaque (see page 14).

STEP 2. With a pencil draw a Wildstyle letter onto the plaque. Use the Plank Method (see page 4) and the diagram above as a guide.

STEP 3. Draw a dark outline around the outside edges of the letter with an Ultra-Fine Point Sharpie or a colored pencil.

STEP 4. Erase the pencil lines with a pink eraser. Rub vigorously.

STEP 5. Draw scribbles all around the outside of the letter (see page 15), or color in with paint, markers, colored pencils or crayons. Finish off with a coat of Varnish if desired.

STEP 6. Glue on rhinestones or sequins to create highlights.

STEP 7. Glue on a popsicle stick shelf (see page 20). Let dry.

STEP 8. Assemble the small ornaments you need (see page 48).

STEP 9. Glue them on and coat with Varnish or Mod Podge.

STEP 10. Attach a hanger or a back stand to display (see page 21).

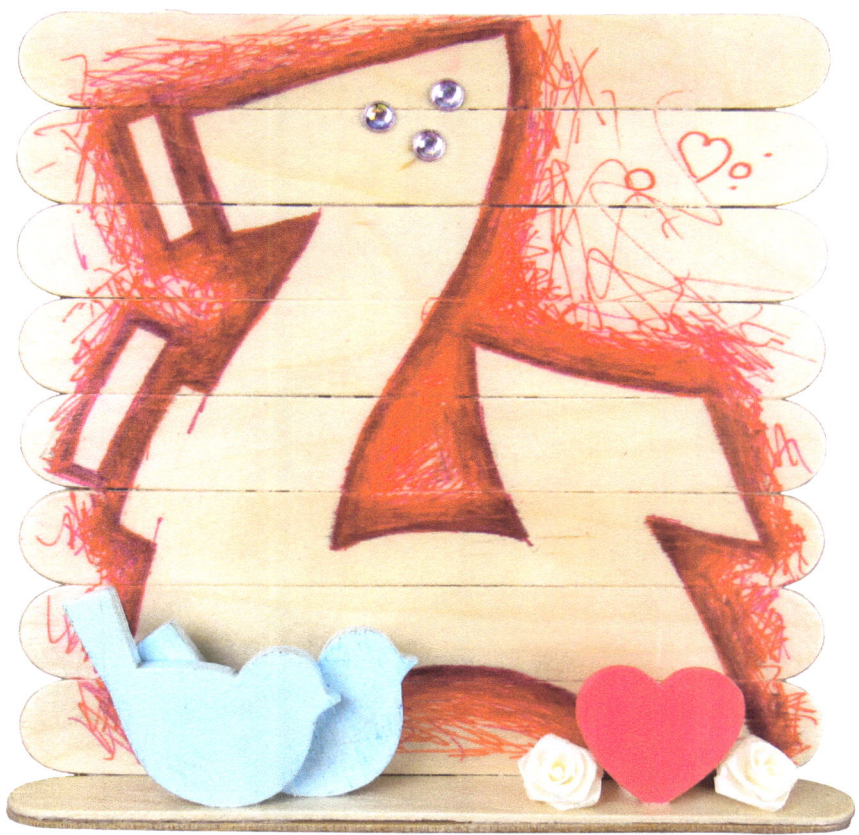

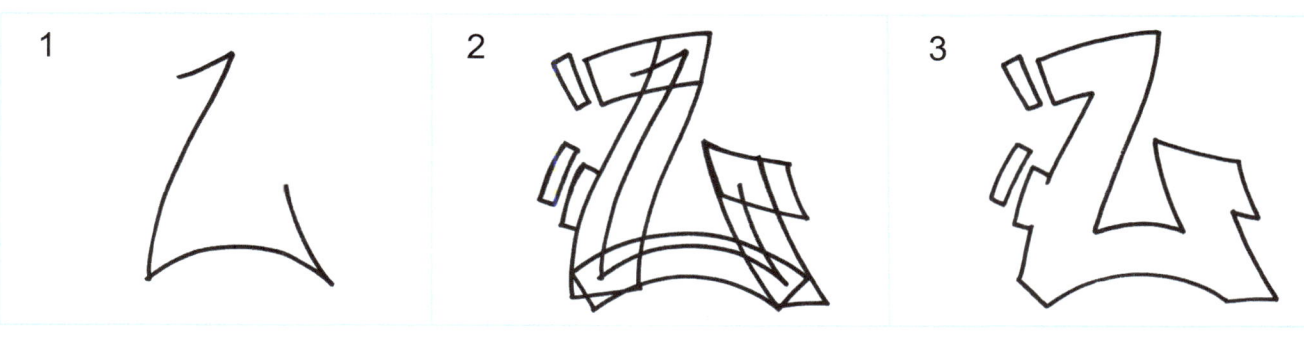

STEP 1. Make a wood plaque (see page 14).
STEP 2. With a pencil draw a Wildstyle letter onto the plaque. Use the Plank Method (see page 4) and the diagram above as a guide.
STEP 3. Draw a dark outline around the outside edges of the letter with an Ultra-Fine Point Sharpie or a colored pencil.
STEP 4. Erase the pencil lines with a pink eraser. Rub vigorously.
STEP 5. Draw scribbles all around the outside of the letter (see page 15), or color in with paint, markers, colored pencils or crayons. Finish off with a coat of Varnish if desired.
STEP 6. Glue on rhinestones or sequins to create highlights.
STEP 7. Glue on a popsicle stick shelf (see page 20). Let dry.
STEP 8. Assemble the small ornaments you need (see page 48).
STEP 9. Glue them on and coat with Varnish or Mod Podge.
STEP 10. Attach a hanger or a back stand to display (see page 21).

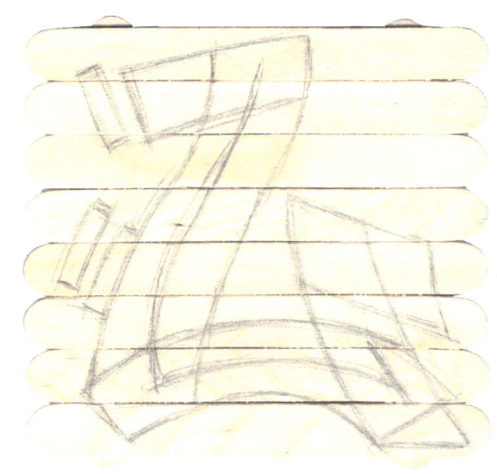

M is for Magnets

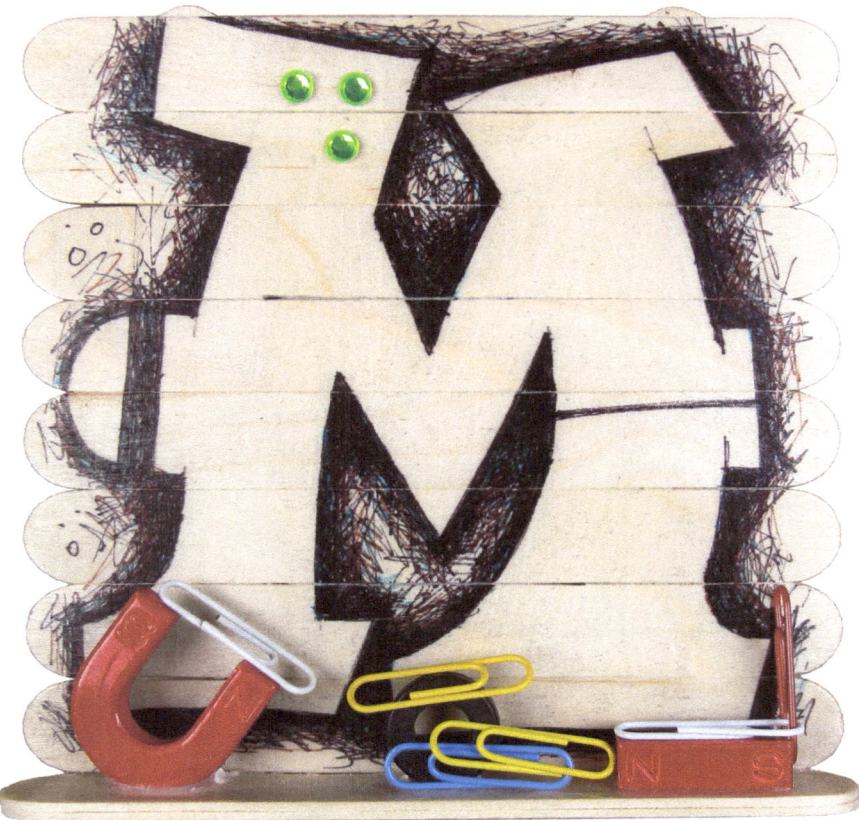

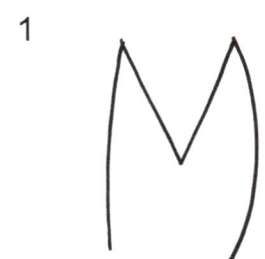 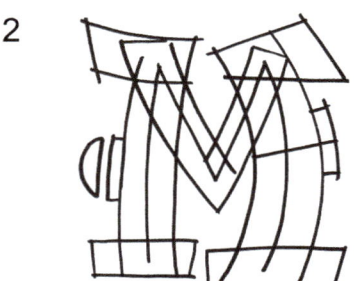 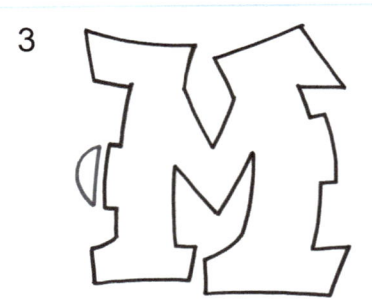

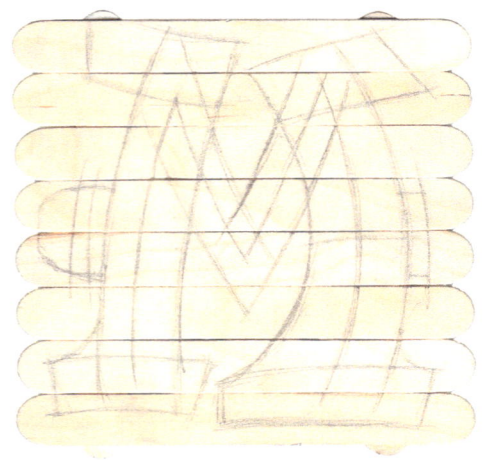

STEP 1. Make a wood plaque (see page 14).
STEP 2. With a pencil draw a Wildstyle letter onto the plaque. Use the Plank Method (see page 4) and the diagram above as a guide.
STEP 3. Draw a dark outline around the outside edges of the letter with an Ultra-Fine Point Sharpie or a colored pencil.
STEP 4. Erase the pencil lines with a pink eraser. Rub vigorously.
STEP 5. Draw scribbles all around the outside of the letter (see page 15), or color in with paint, markers, colored pencils or crayons. Finish off with a coat of Varnish if desired.
STEP 6. Glue on rhinestones or sequins to create highlights.
STEP 7. Glue on a popsicle stick shelf (see page 20). Let dry.
STEP 8. Assemble the small ornaments you need (see page 48).
STEP 9. Glue them on and coat with Varnish or Mod Podge.
STEP 10. Attach a hanger or a back stand to display (see page 21).

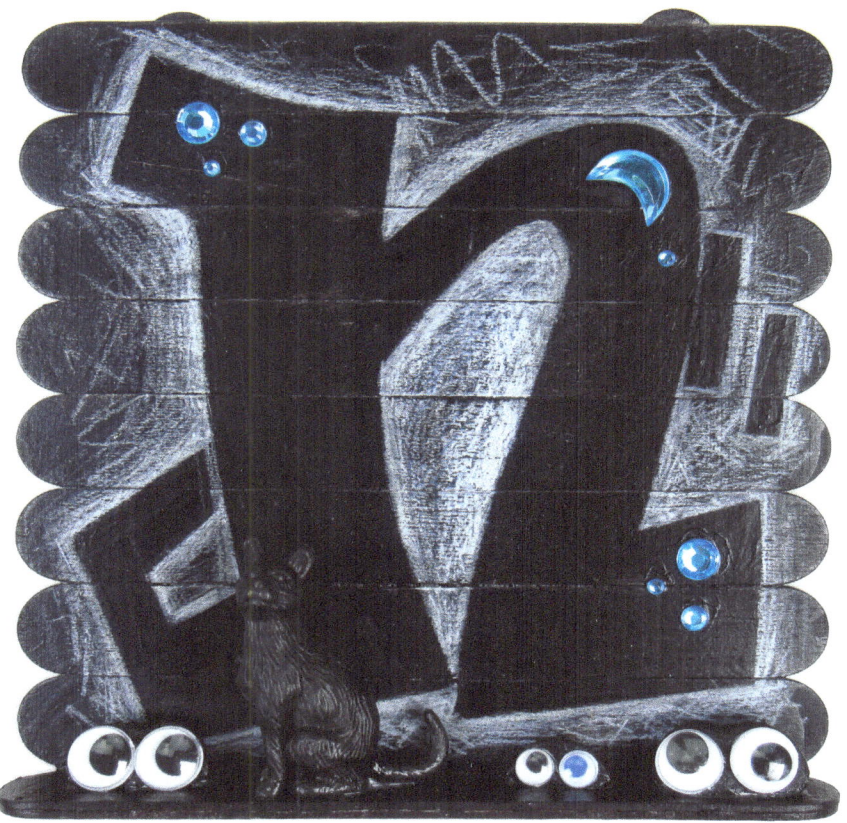

To make these wiggly-eyed monsters, see page 51.

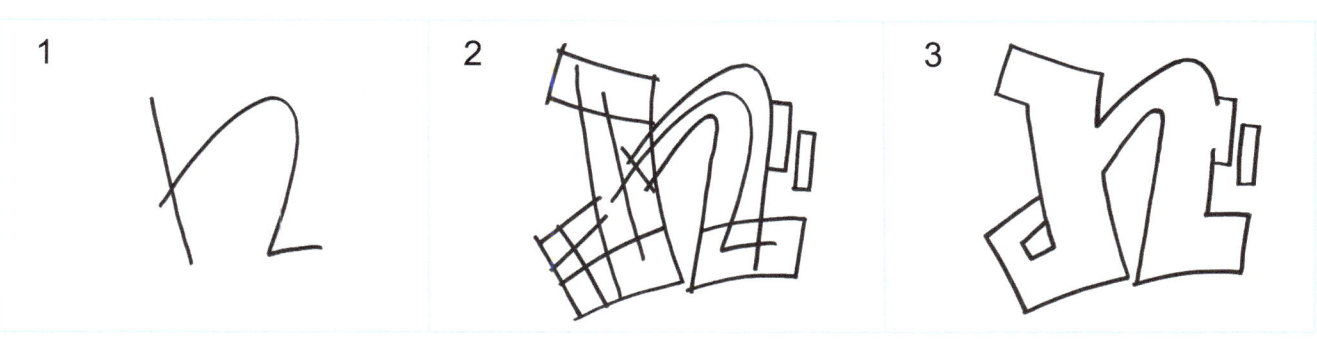

STEP 1. Make a wood plaque (see page 14).
STEP 2. You can decorate this plaque following the instructions on page 16. Or color it the same way as the other alphabet projects.
STEP 3. Glue on rhinestones or sequins to create highlights.
STEP 4. Glue on a popsicle stick shelf (see page 20). Let dry.
STEP 5. Assemble the small ornaments you need (see page 48).
STEP 6. Glue them on and coat with Varnish or Mod Podge.
STEP 7. Attach a hanger or a back stand to display (see page 21).

You can use the Uppercase letter N from page 11 in place of the lowercase letter n above.

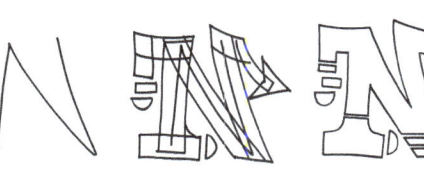

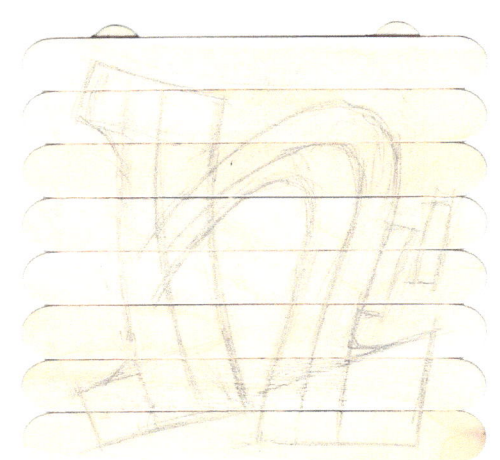

O is for Orange

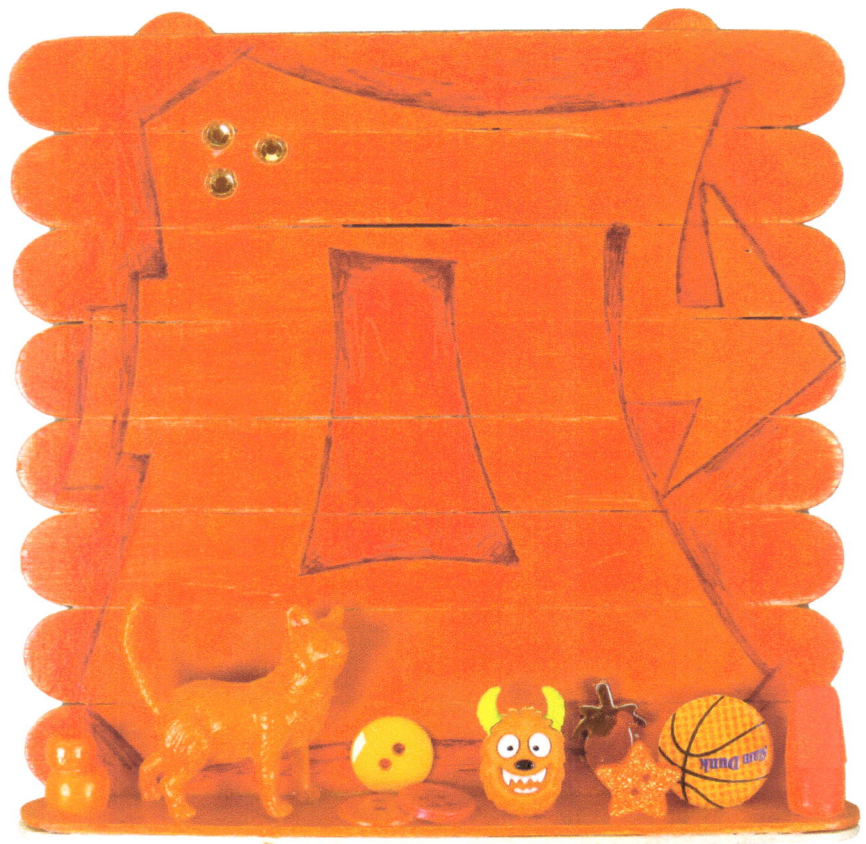

I used a pre-made monster button but you can make your own monster with the instructions on page 51.

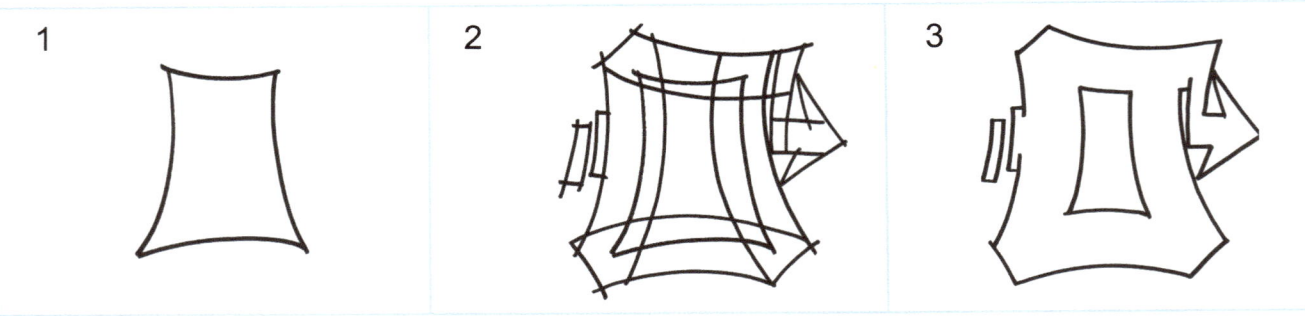

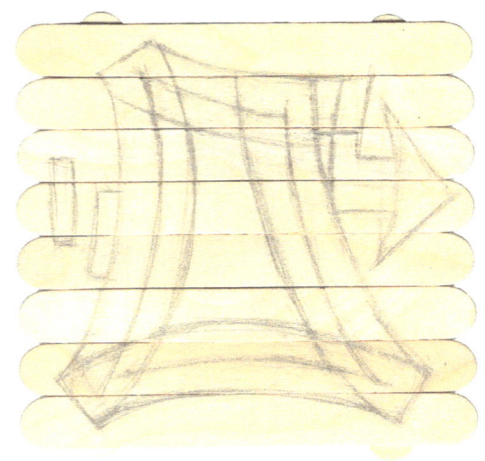

STEP 1. Make a wood plaque (see page 14).
STEP 2. With a pencil draw a Wildstyle letter onto the plaque. Use the Plank Method (see page 4) and the diagram above as a guide.
STEP 3. Draw a dark outline around the outside edges of the letter with an Ultra-Fine Point Sharpie or a colored pencil.
STEP 4. Erase the pencil lines with a pink eraser. Rub vigorously.
STEP 5. You can paint this plaque following the instructions on pages 18-19. Or decorate it any other way you like.
STEP 6. Glue on rhinestones or sequins to create highlights.
STEP 7. Glue on a popsicle stick shelf (see page 20). Let dry.
STEP 8. Assemble the small ornaments you need (see page 48).
STEP 9. Glue them on and coat with Varnish or Mod Podge.
STEP 10. Attach a hanger or a back stand to display (see page 21).

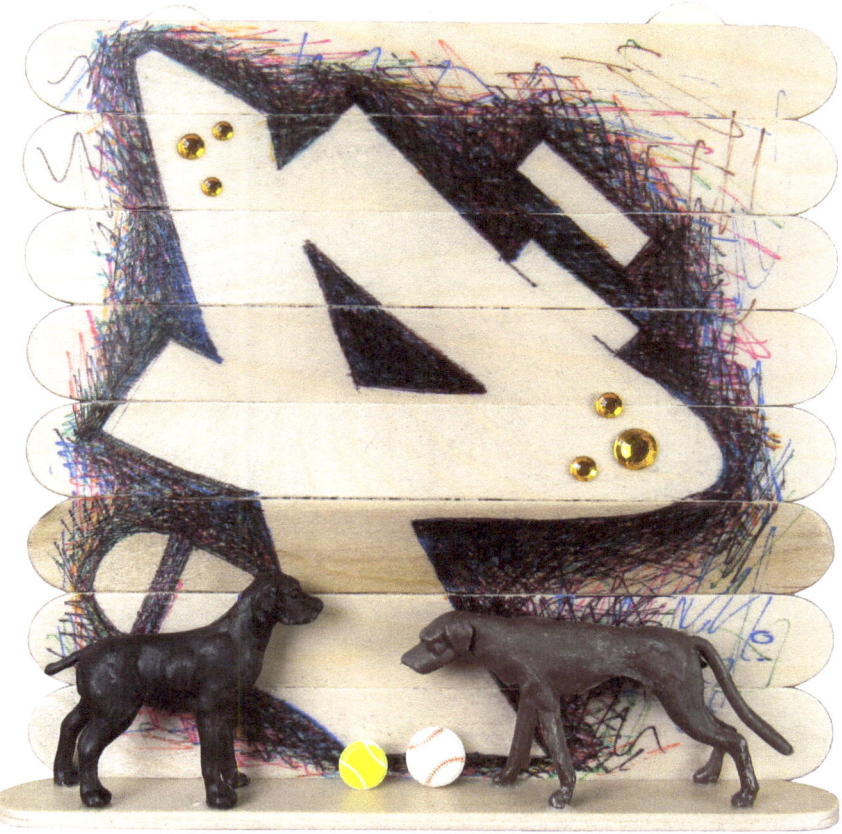

The baseball and tennis ball are made from small stickers with air-dry clay on the back. See page 54.

1	2	3

STEP 1. Make a wood plaque (see page 14).

STEP 2. With a pencil draw a Wildstyle letter onto the plaque. Use the Plank Method (see page 4) and the diagram above as a guide.

STEP 3. Draw a dark outline around the outside edges of the letter with an Ultra-Fine Point Sharpie or a colored pencil.

STEP 4. Erase the pencil lines with a pink eraser. Rub vigorously.

STEP 5. Draw scribbles all around the outside of the letter (see page 15), or color in with paint, markers, colored pencils or crayons. Finish off with a coat of Varnish if desired.

STEP 6. Glue on rhinestones or sequins to create highlights.

STEP 7. Glue on a popsicle stick shelf (see page 20). Let dry.

STEP 8. Assemble the small ornaments you need (see page 48).

STEP 9. Glue them on and coat with Varnish or Mod Podge.

STEP 10. Attach a hanger or a back stand to display (see page 21).

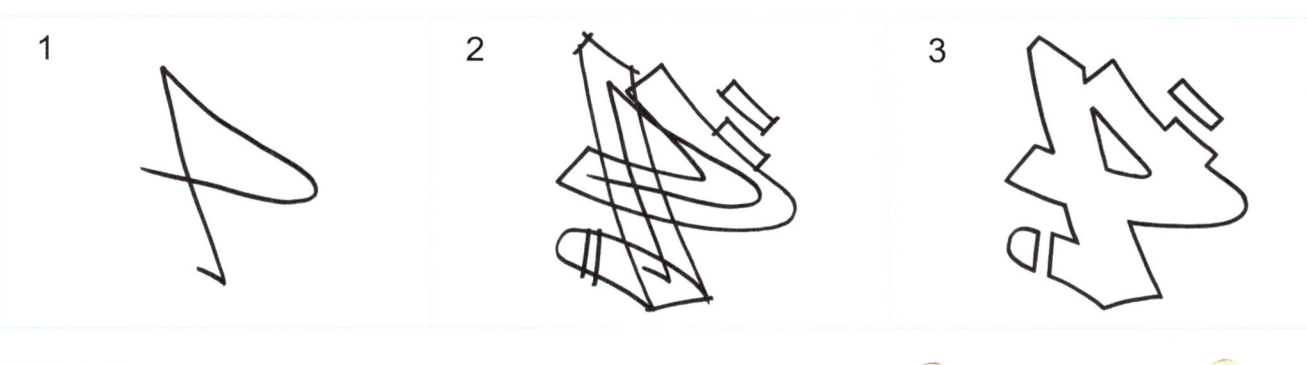

Q is for Quintuplets

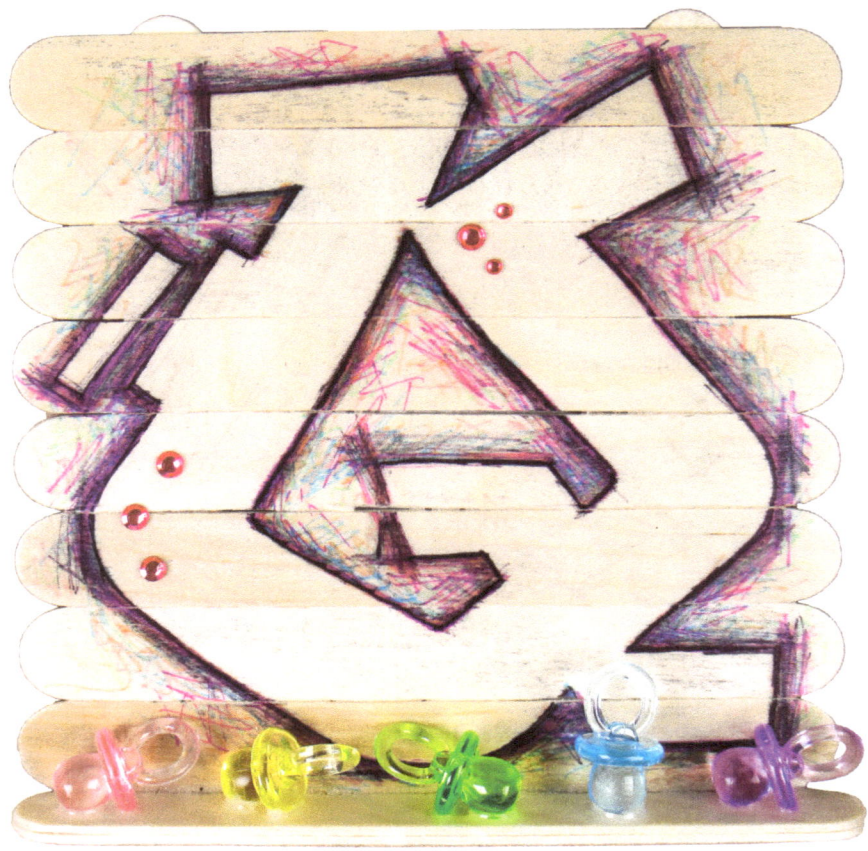

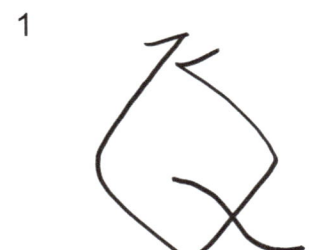 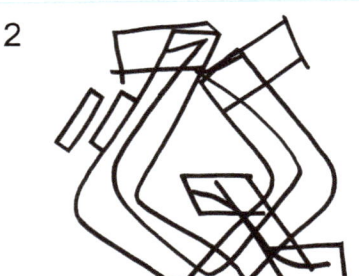 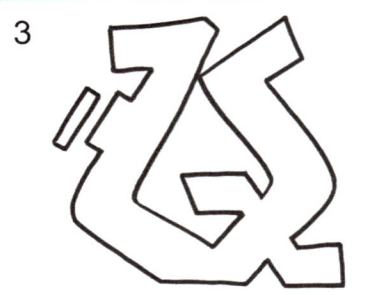

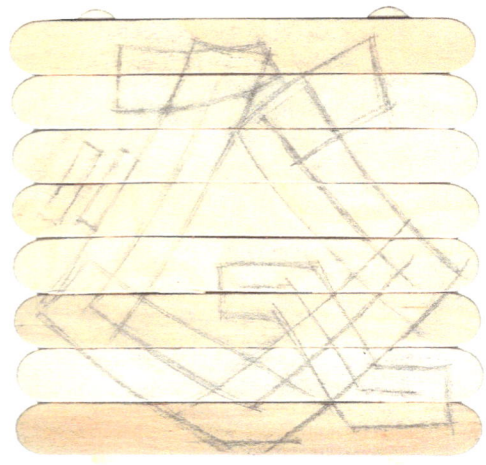

STEP 1. Make a wood plaque (see page 14).

STEP 2. With a pencil draw a Wildstyle letter onto the plaque. Use the Plank Method (see page 4) and the diagram above as a guide.

STEP 3. Draw a dark outline around the outside edges of the letter with an Ultra-Fine Point Sharpie or a colored pencil.

STEP 4. Erase the pencil lines with a pink eraser. Rub vigorously.

STEP 5. Draw scribbles all around the outside of the letter (see page 15), or color in with paint, markers, colored pencils or crayons. Finish off with a coat of Varnish if desired.

STEP 6. Glue on rhinestones or sequins to create highlights.

STEP 7. Glue on a popsicle stick shelf (see page 20). Let dry.

STEP 8. Assemble the small ornaments you need (see page 48).

STEP 9. Glue them on and coat with Varnish or Mod Podge.

STEP 10. Attach a hanger or a back stand to display (see page 21).

R is for Rock Painting (and Rabbit)

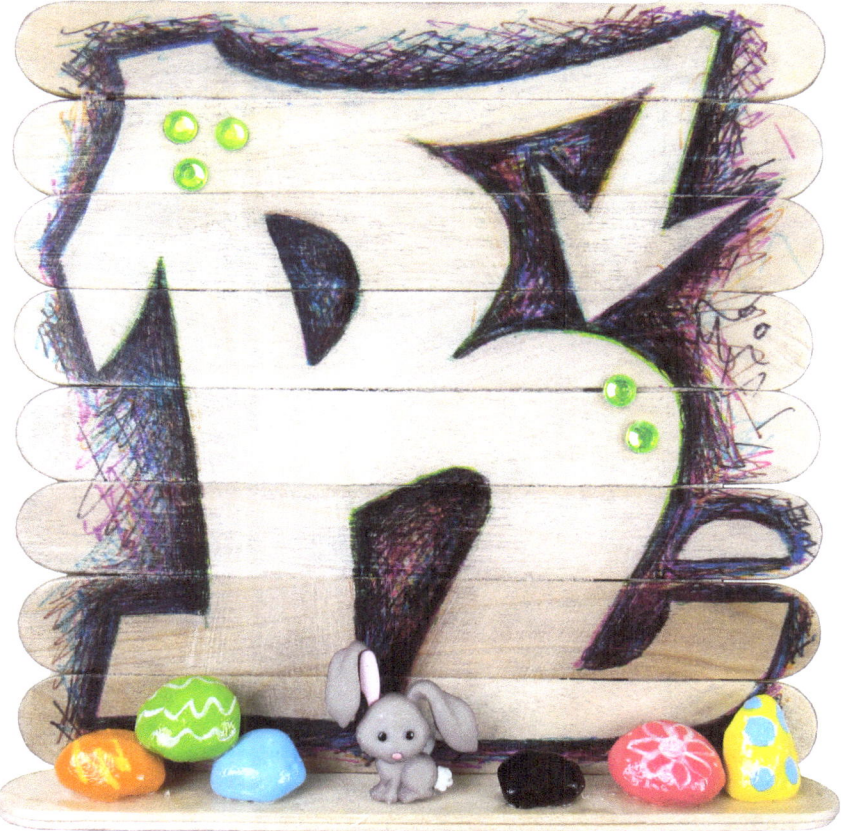

The rabbit is a plastic button from a craft store with a bead glued on back to make it stand up. See page 54. To make painted rocks, see page 49.

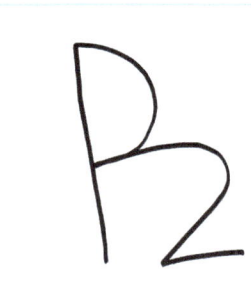

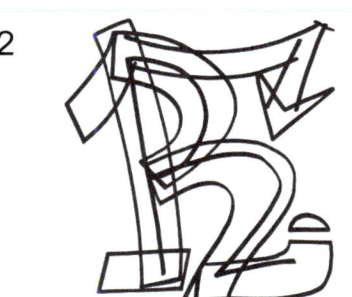

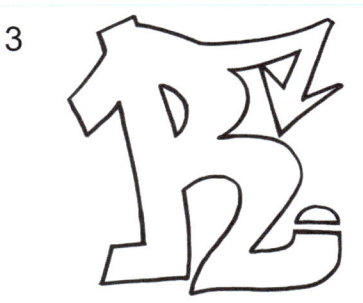

STEP 1. Make a wood plaque (see page 14).
STEP 2. With a pencil draw a Wildstyle letter onto the plaque. Use the Plank Method (see page 4) and the diagram above as a guide.
STEP 3. Draw a dark outline around the outside edges of the letter with an Ultra-Fine Point Sharpie or a colored pencil.
STEP 4. Erase the pencil lines with a pink eraser. Rub vigorously.
STEP 5. Draw scribbles all around the outside of the letter (see page 15), or color in with paint, markers, colored pencils or crayons. Finish off with a coat of Varnish if desired.
STEP 6. Glue on rhinestones or sequins to create highlights.
STEP 7. Glue on a popsicle stick shelf (see page 20). Let dry.
STEP 8. Assemble the small ornaments you need (see page 48).
STEP 9. Glue them on and coat with Varnish or Mod Podge.
STEP 10. Attach a hanger or a back stand to display (see page 21).

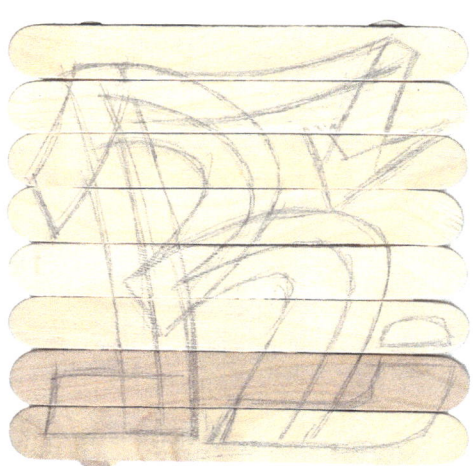

S is for Sea Glass

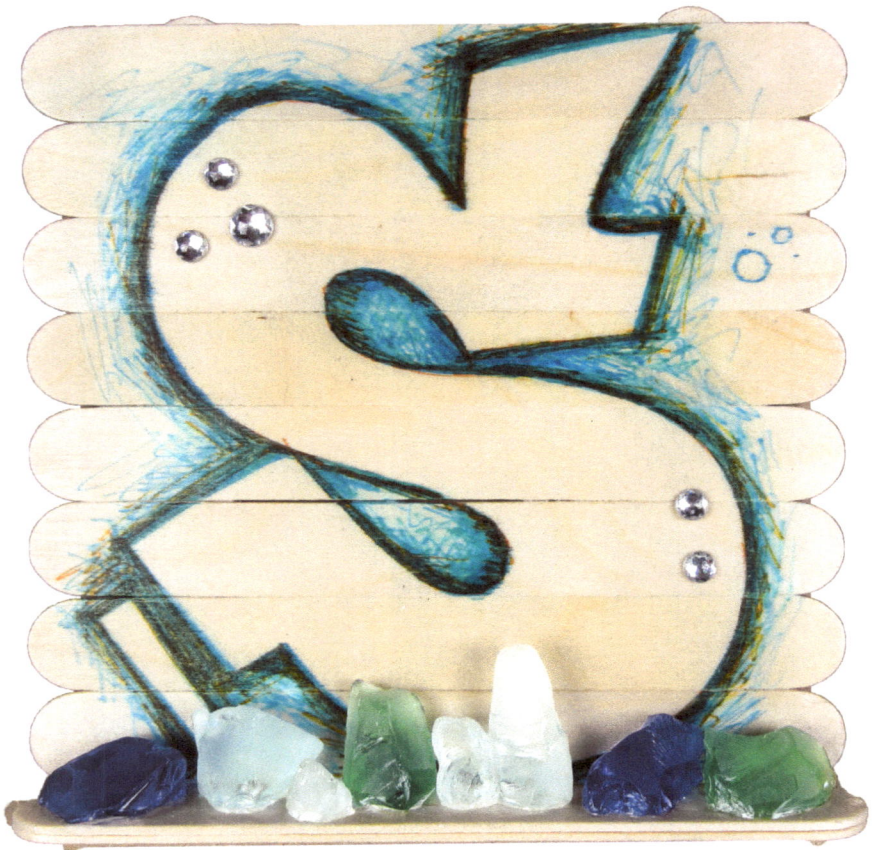

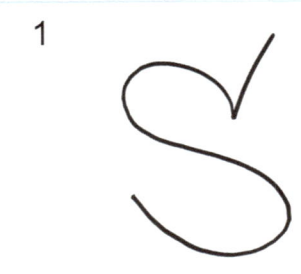

1
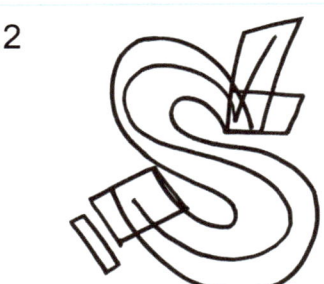

2 3

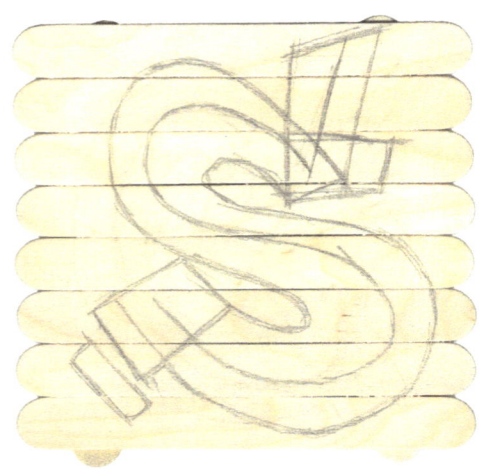

STEP 1. Make a wood plaque (see page 14).
STEP 2. With a pencil draw a Wildstyle letter onto the plaque. Use the Plank Method (see page 4) and the diagram above as a guide.
STEP 3. Draw a dark outline around the outside edges of the letter with an Ultra-Fine Point Sharpie or a colored pencil.
STEP 4. Erase the pencil lines with a pink eraser. Rub vigorously.
STEP 5. Draw scribbles all around the outside of the letter (see page 15), or color in with paint, markers, colored pencils or crayons. Finish off with a coat of Varnish if desired.
STEP 6. Glue on rhinestones or sequins to create highlights.
STEP 7. Glue on a popsicle stick shelf (see page 20). Let dry.
STEP 8. Assemble the small ornaments you need (see page 48).
STEP 9. Glue them on and coat with Varnish or Mod Podge.
STEP 10. Attach a hanger or a back stand to display (see page 21).

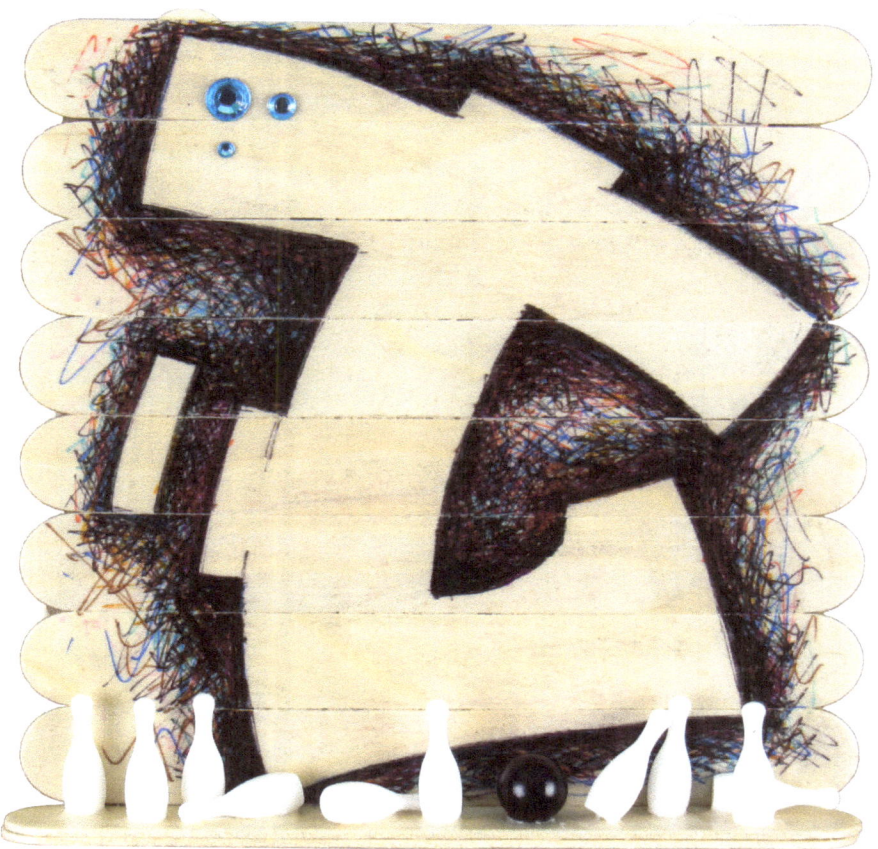

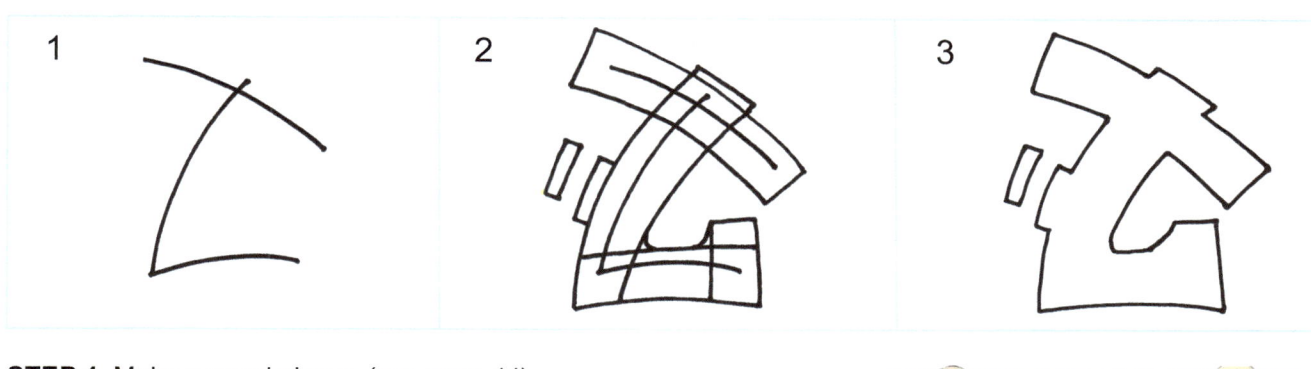

STEP 1. Make a wood plaque (see page 14).

STEP 2. With a pencil draw a Wildstyle letter onto the plaque. Use the Plank Method (see page 4) and the diagram above as a guide.

STEP 3. Draw a dark outline around the outside edges of the letter with an Ultra-Fine Point Sharpie or a colored pencil.

STEP 4. Erase the pencil lines with a pink eraser. Rub vigorously.

STEP 5. Draw scribbles all around the outside of the letter (see page 15), or color in with paint, markers, colored pencils or crayons. Finish off with a coat of Varnish if desired.

STEP 6. Glue on rhinestones or sequins to create highlights.

STEP 7. Glue on a popsicle stick shelf (see page 20). Let dry.

STEP 8. Assemble the small ornaments you need (see page 48).

STEP 9. Glue them on and coat with Varnish or Mod Podge.

STEP 10. Attach a hanger or a back stand to display (see page 21).

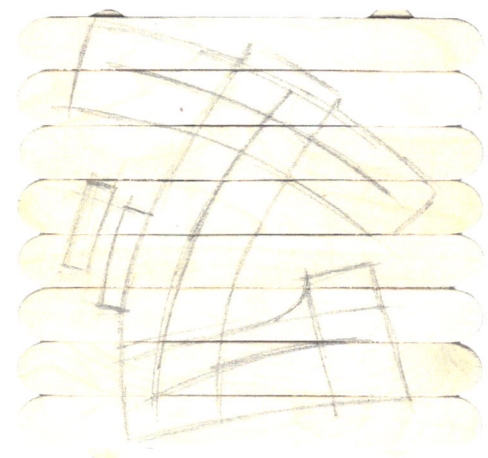

U is for Upside-down

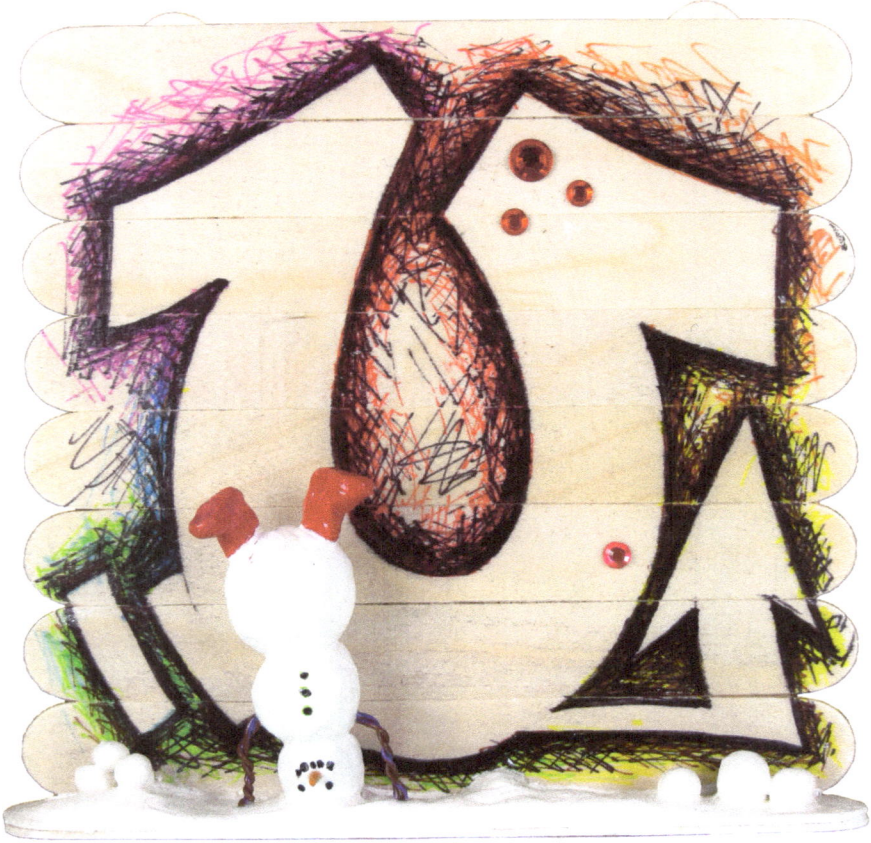

The snowman, snow, and snowballs are made with air-dry clay. See page 53.

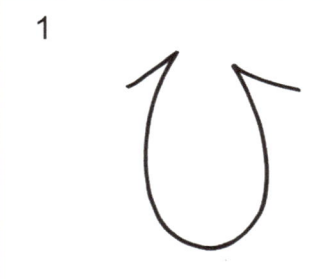

1

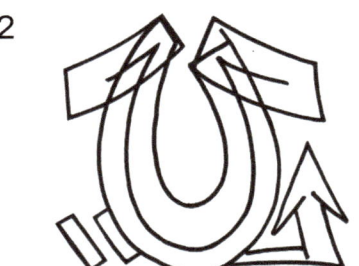

2

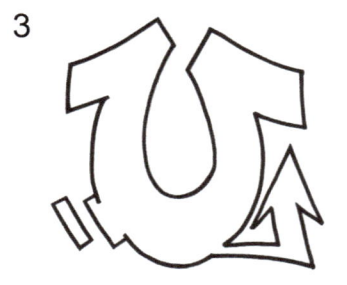

3

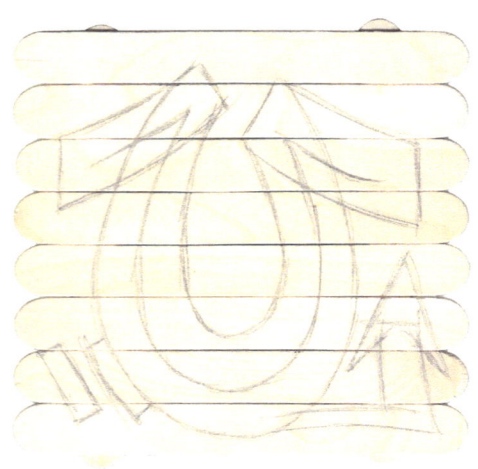

STEP 1. Make a wood plaque (see page 14).

STEP 2. With a pencil draw a Wildstyle letter onto the plaque. Use the Plank Method (see page 4) and the diagram above as a guide.

STEP 3. Draw a dark outline around the outside edges of the letter with an Ultra-Fine Point Sharpie or a colored pencil.

STEP 4. Erase the pencil lines with a pink eraser. Rub vigorously.

STEP 5. Draw scribbles all around the outside of the letter (see page 15), or color in with paint, markers, colored pencils or crayons. Finish off with a coat of Varnish if desired.

STEP 6. Glue on rhinestones or sequins to create highlights.

STEP 7. Glue on a popsicle stick shelf (see page 20). Let dry.

STEP 8. Assemble the small ornaments you need (see page 48).

STEP 9. Glue them on and coat with Varnish or Mod Podge.

STEP 10. Attach a hanger or a back stand to display (see page 21).

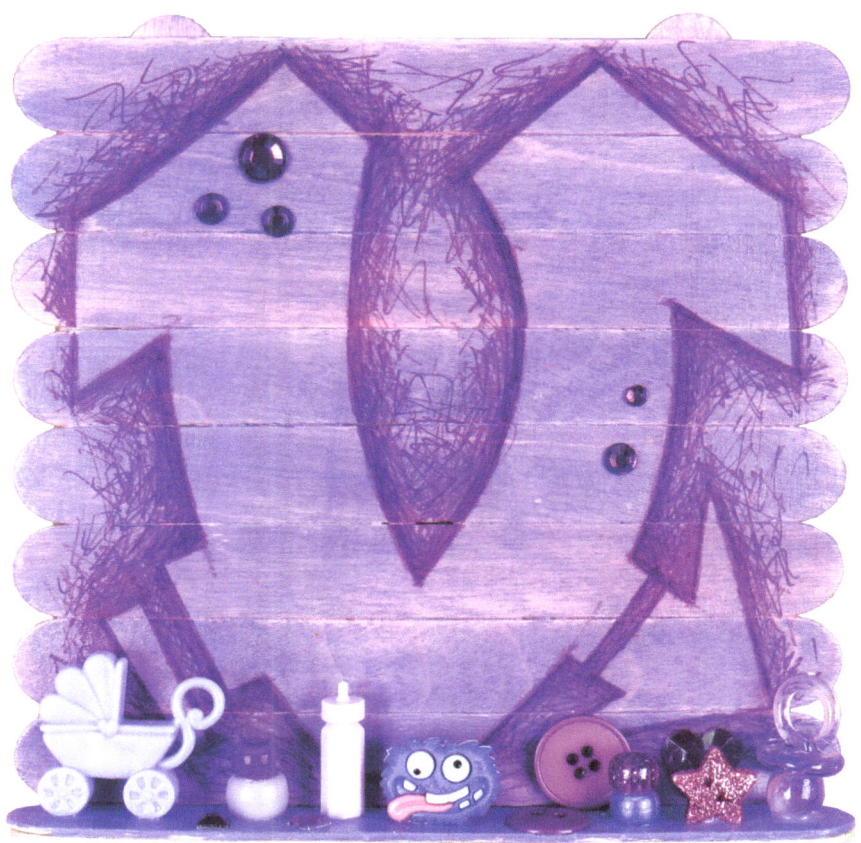

I used a pre-made monster button but you can make your own monster with the instructions on page 51.

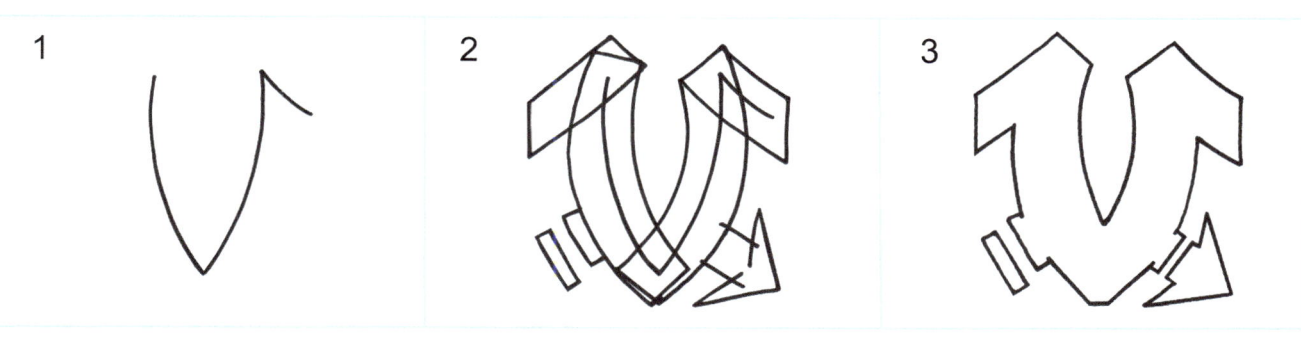

1 2 3

STEP 1. Make a wood plaque (see page 14).

STEP 2. With a pencil draw a Wildstyle letter onto the plaque. Use the Plank Method (see page 4) and the diagram above as a guide.

STEP 3. Draw a dark outline around the outside edges of the letter with an Ultra-Fine Point Sharpie or a colored pencil.

STEP 4. Erase the pencil lines with a pink eraser. Rub vigorously.

STEP 5. You can paint this plaque following the instructions on pages 18-19. Or decorate it any other way you like.

STEP 6. Glue on rhinestones or sequins to create highlights.

STEP 7. Glue on a popsicle stick shelf (see page 20). Let dry.

STEP 8. Assemble the small ornaments you need (see page 48).

STEP 9. Glue them on and coat with Varnish or Mod Podge.

STEP 10. Attach a hanger or a back stand to display (see page 21).

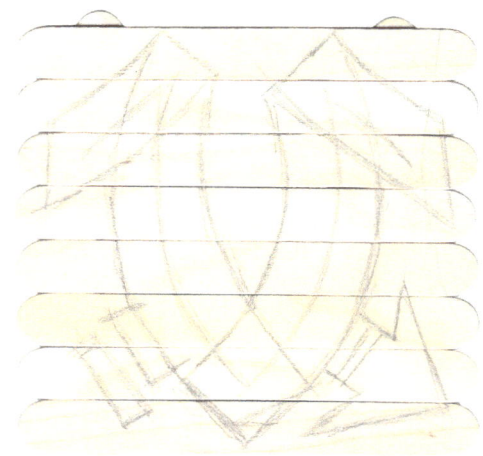

W is for Woodland Animals

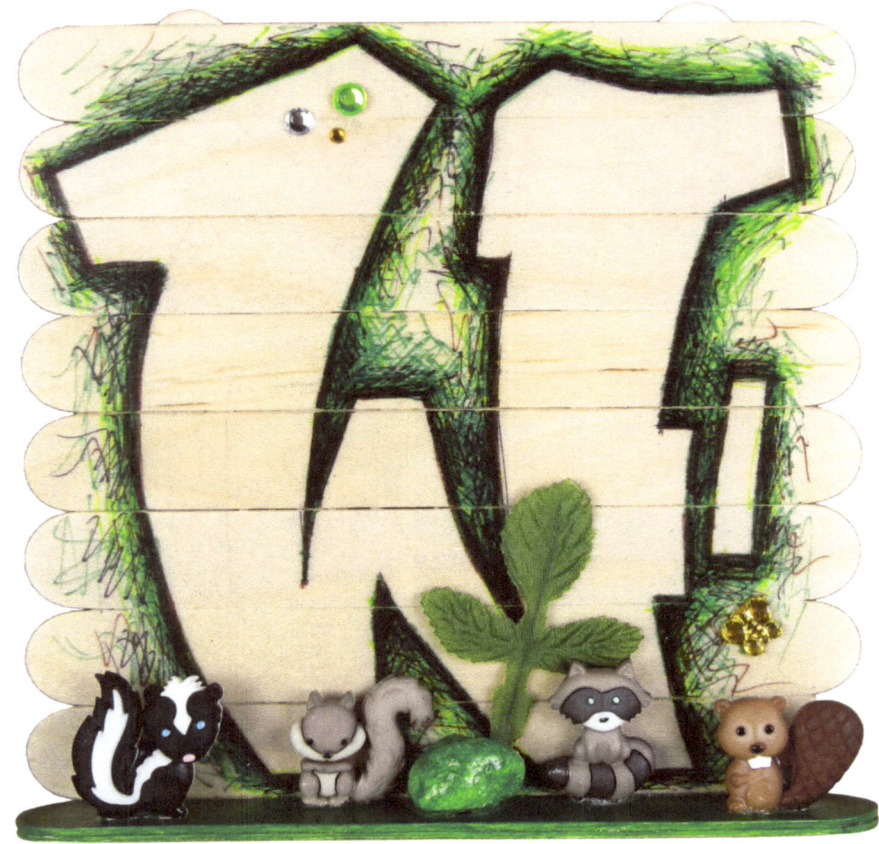

These Woodland animals are buttons from a craft store with the loops removed and plastic beads glued on back to make them stand up. See page 54.

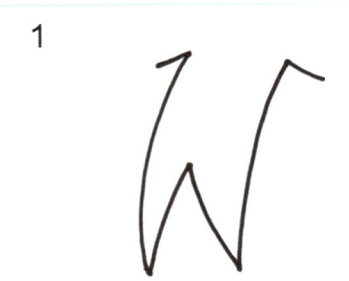

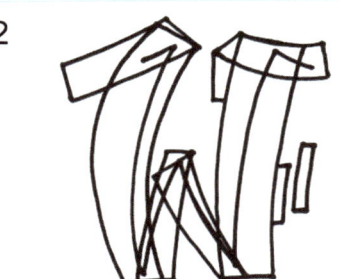

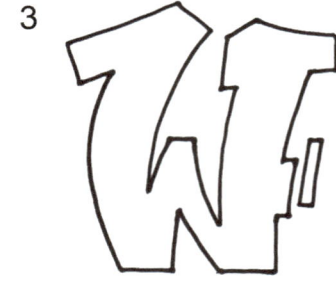

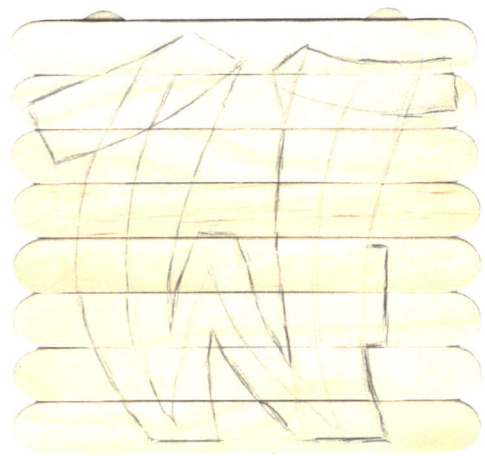

STEP 1. Make a wood plaque (see page 14).
STEP 2. With a pencil draw a Wildstyle letter onto the plaque. Use the Plank Method (see page 4) and the diagram above as a guide.
STEP 3. Draw a dark outline around the outside edges of the letter with an Ultra-Fine Point Sharpie or a colored pencil.
STEP 4. Erase the pencil lines with a pink eraser. Rub vigorously.
STEP 5. Draw scribbles all around the outside of the letter (see page 15), or color in with paint, markers, colored pencils or crayons. Finish off with a coat of Varnish if desired.
STEP 6. Glue on rhinestones or sequins to create highlights.
STEP 7. Glue on a popsicle stick shelf (see page 20). Let dry.
STEP 8. Assemble the small ornaments you need (see page 48).
STEP 9. Glue them on and coat with Varnish or Mod Podge.
STEP 10. Attach a hanger or a back stand to display (see page 21).

X is for Xylophone

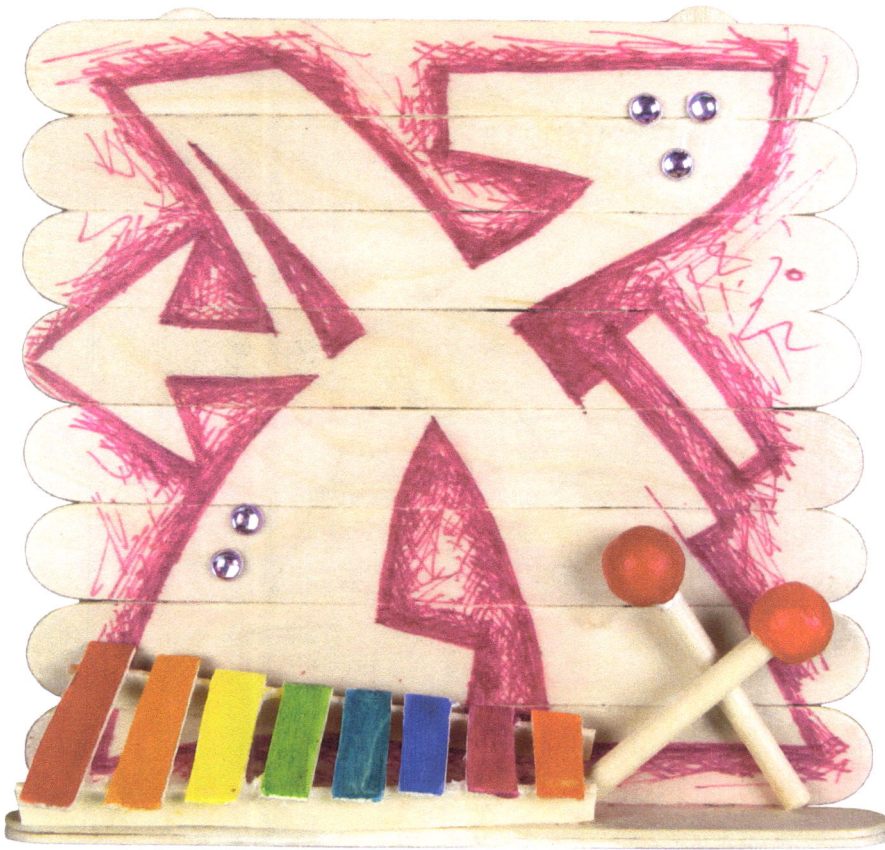

The Xylophone is made with regular size popsicle sticks. See page 55. It is a bit large. You can glue it on on an angle or just lean it against the front.

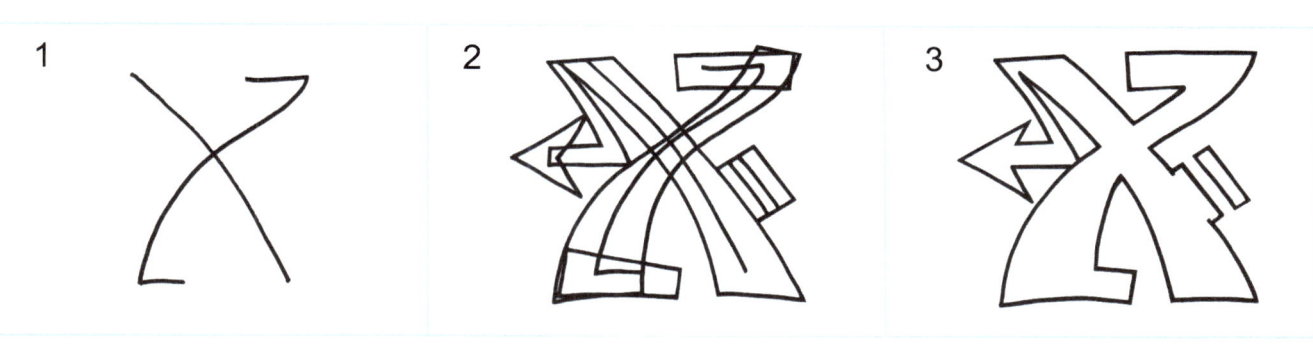

1

2

3

STEP 1. Make a wood plaque (see page 14).
STEP 2. With a pencil draw a Wildstyle letter onto the plaque. Use the Plank Method (see page 4) and the diagram above as a guide.
STEP 3. Draw a dark outline around the outside edges of the letter with an Ultra-Fine Point Sharpie or a colored pencil.
STEP 4. Erase the pencil lines with a pink eraser. Rub vigorously.
STEP 5. Draw scribbles all around the outside of the letter (see page 15), or color in with paint, markers, colored pencils or crayons. Finish off with a coat of Varnish if desired.
STEP 6. Glue on rhinestones or sequins to create highlights.
STEP 7. Glue on a popsicle stick shelf (see page 20). Let dry.
STEP 8. Assemble the small ornaments you need (see page 48).
STEP 9. Glue them on and coat with Varnish or Mod Podge.
STEP 10. Attach a hanger or a back stand to display (see page 21).

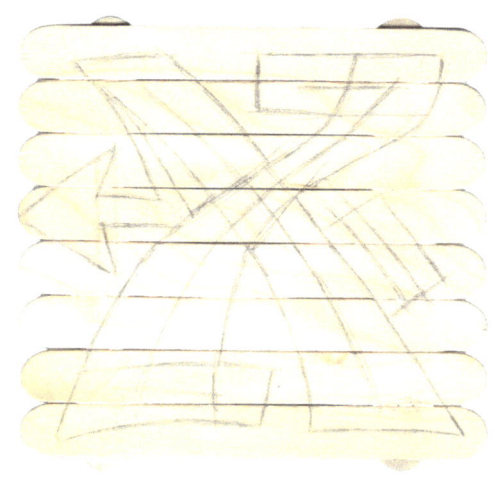

Y is for Yoyo

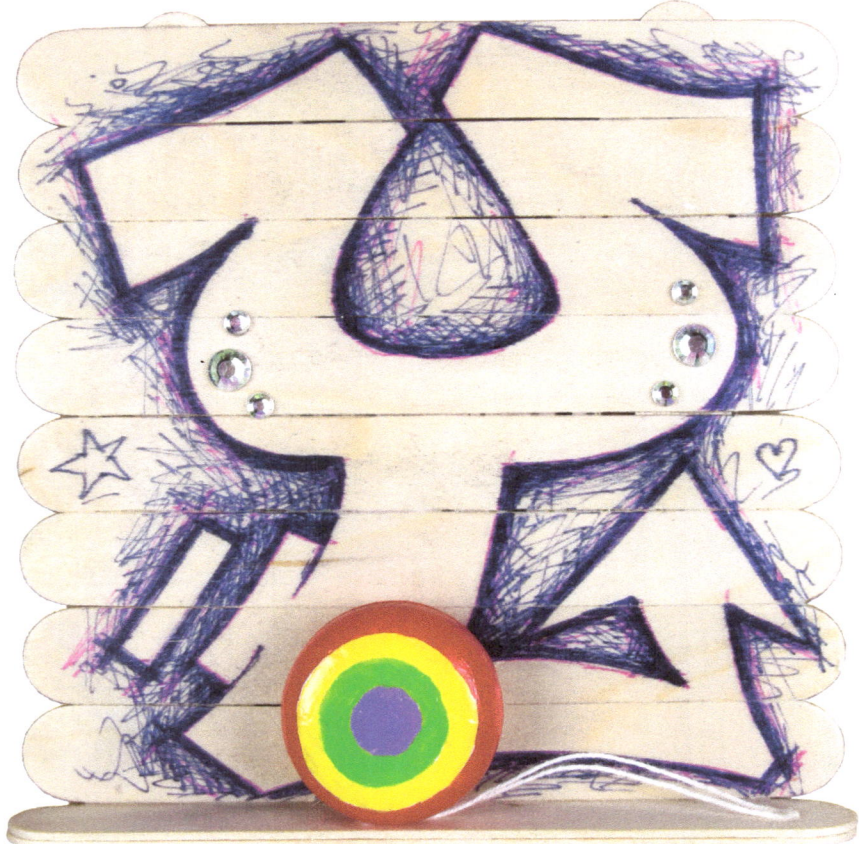

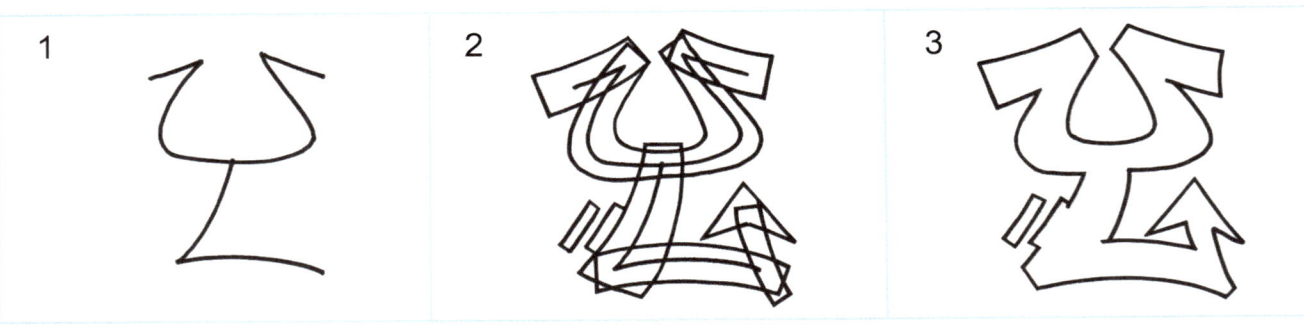

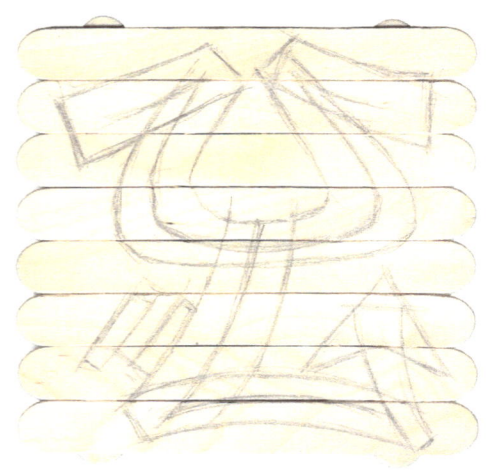

STEP 1. Make a wood plaque (see page 14).
STEP 2. With a pencil draw a Wildstyle letter onto the plaque. Use the Plank Method (see page 4) and the diagram above as a guide.
STEP 3. Draw a dark outline around the outside edges of the letter with an Ultra-Fine Point Sharpie or a colored pencil.
STEP 4. Erase the pencil lines with a pink eraser. Rub vigorously.
STEP 5. Draw scribbles all around the outside of the letter (see page 15), or color in with paint, markers, colored pencils or crayons. Finish off with a coat of Varnish if desired.
STEP 6. Glue on rhinestones or sequins to create highlights.
STEP 7. Glue on a popsicle stick shelf (see page 20). Let dry.
STEP 8. Assemble the small ornaments you need (see page 48).
STEP 9. Glue them on and coat with Varnish or Mod Podge.
STEP 10. Attach a hanger or a back stand to display (see page 21).

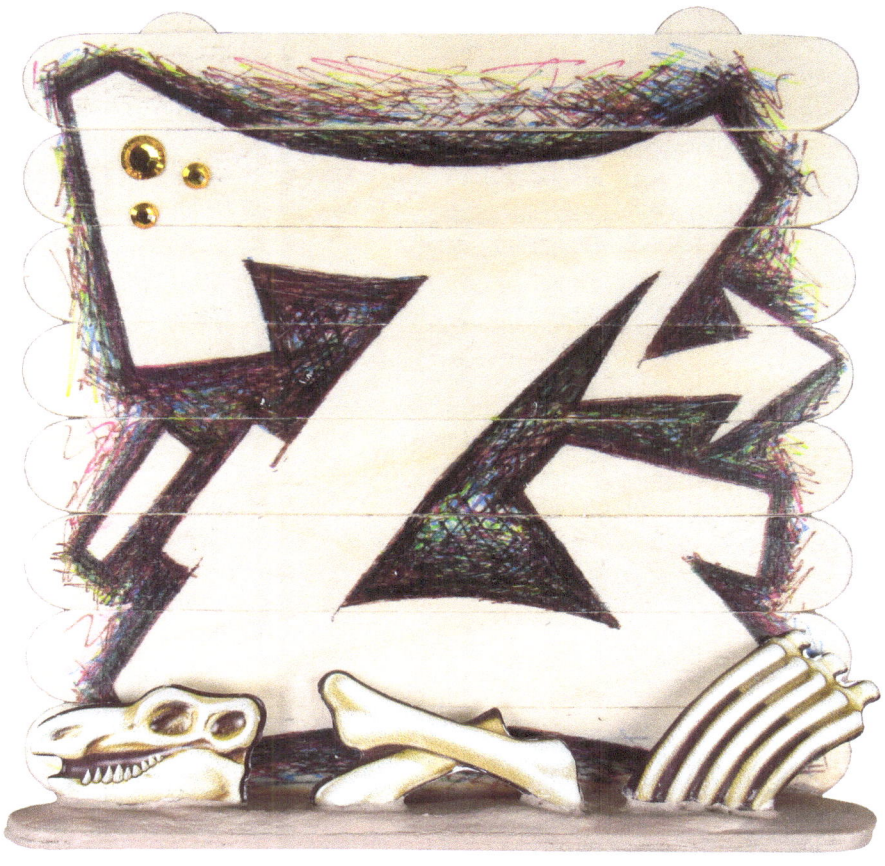

These dino-saur bones are made from store bought plastic stickers and backed with air-dry clay to make them three-dimensional. See page 54.

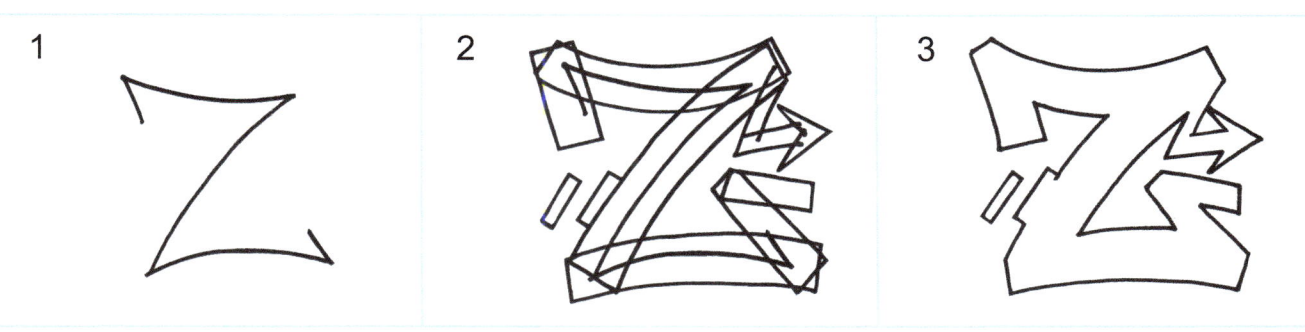

1　2　3

STEP 1. Make a wood plaque (see page 14).
STEP 2. With a pencil draw a Wildstyle letter onto the plaque. Use the Plank Method (see page 4) and the diagram above as a guide.
STEP 3. Draw a dark outline around the outside edges of the letter with an Ultra-Fine Point Sharpie or a colored pencil.
STEP 4. Erase the pencil lines with a pink eraser. Rub vigorously.
STEP 5. Draw scribbles all around the outside of the letter (see page 15), or color in with paint, markers, colored pencils or crayons. Finish off with a coat of Varnish if desired.
STEP 6. Glue on rhinestones or sequins to create highlights.
STEP 7. Glue on a popsicle stick shelf (see page 20). Let dry.
STEP 8. Assemble the small ornaments you need (see page 48).
STEP 9. Glue them on and coat with Varnish or Mod Podge.
STEP 10. Attach a hanger or a back stand to display (see page 21).

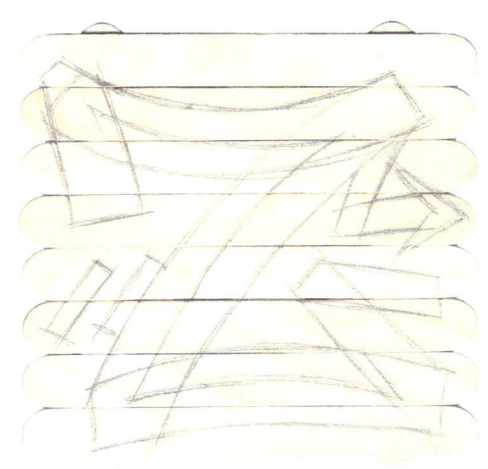

PART FOUR: ATTACHING ORNAMENTS

All of the ornaments used to decorate the projects in this book were purchased at a local dollar store, a craft store, or a big box department store. You don't need expensive materials to make a popsicle stick graffiti project. You can use shells, toothpicks, leaves, felt, foam, rhinestones, sequins, rocks, party favors, miniature flowers, beads, wiggly eyes, stickers, office supplies, wood cutouts, magnets, you name it. Come up with your own ideas. Craft stores and dollar stores sell just about everything you can think of and you don't have to spend a lot of money at all. You can use everyday household objects as well, such as buttons. Or try screws, nuts, and bolts from your toolbox. You can make small ornaments from air-dry clay which is sold inexpensively at craft and art supply stores. Air-dry clay dries quickly and can be colored with water-soluble acrylic paints. I recommend using Tacky glue which can be purchased at craft stores. Multi-purpose white glue can be used instead.

WHAT YOU NEED • Ornaments • Tacky Glue or White Glue • Mod Podge or Varnish • Paint brush

1 The best way to attach the ornaments you need to the popsicle stick shelf is to glue them on with <u>extra thick tacky glue</u>. Regular white glue may not bond as well to some types of plastic objects. Tacky glue dries clear so it will not affect the look of your finished artwork.

2 This trick will ensure your projects last a lifetime. With a small brush paint around the base of the ornaments with Mod Podge or Varnish. This will fasten them securely to the wood shelf. Make sure the Mod Podge or Varnish touches both the object and the shelf.

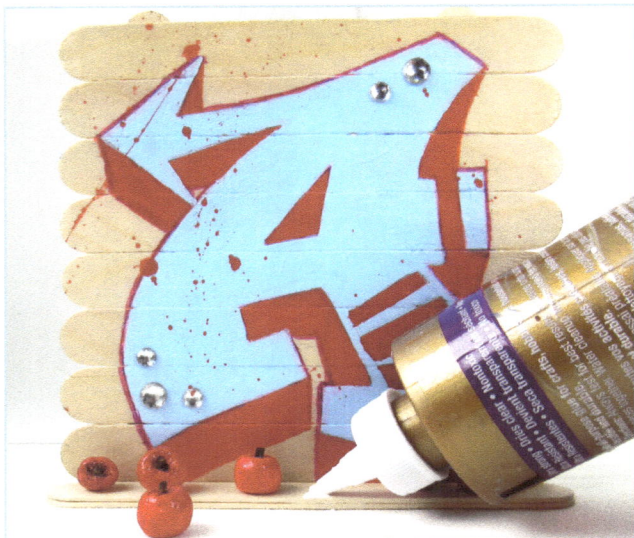
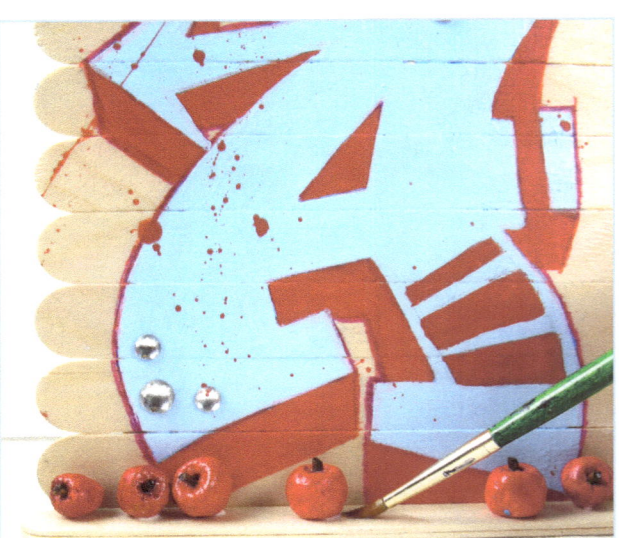

ORNAMENTS USED TO DECORATE THE PROJECTS FROM A to Z

A - Miniature apples made from air-dry clay and toothpicks. Tiny wooden crate made from popsicle sticks. See page 50 for instructions. You can skip the crate and just make the apples.

B - Assorted buttons from the craft store and from old shirts and blouses.

C - Conch shells from the dollar store. Coral paper sticker from the dollar store.

D - Plastic dinosaurs from the dollar store.

E - Package of erasers from the dollar store.

F - Miniature silk flowers from the craft store. Beads from a big box department store or toy store.

G - Use an assortment of green objects. For this project, I used a pre-made monster button from the craft store but you can make a homemade mini monster with air-dry clay by following the instructions on page 51.

H - Pumpkin and Candy Corn made with air-dry clay. Bats from the dollar store. The tree is cut from a branch.

I - Plastic spider from the dollar store. Bag of lady bugs from the craft store.

J - Plastic rhinestones from the big box department store.

K - Paper Keyboard on page 54.

L - Wooden heart and birds from the craft store. Miniature flowers from the craft store.

M - Small magnets from the toy store.

N - Monsters with wiggly eyes made from air-dry clay. Plastic cat from dollar store. See instructions on page 51.

O - Assorted orange objects: beads, buttons, sticker, eraser, plastic cat, monster button (see page 51).

P - Plastic dogs from the dollar store. Little balls are stickers backed with air-dry clay (see page 54).

Q - Plastic pacifiers from the dollar store.

R - Rocks painted with acrylic paint (see below). Rabbit button glued to a bead (see page 54).

S - Sea glass from the dollar store.

T - Plastic bowling pins from the party store.

U - Air-dry clay snowman, snowballs, and snow drifts (see page 53).

V - Assorted violet objects: buttons, beads, baby party favors, rhinestones, etc.

W - Woodland animal buttons from the craft store (see page 54).

X - Xylophone made from regular size popsicle sticks. Mallets made with wood barbecue sticks from the grocery store and air-dry clay.

Y - The plastic yoyo is a party favor from the dollar store. I painted over it with acrylic paint to make it colorful.

Z - Dinosaurs made from plastic puffy stickers. Backed with air-dry clay (see page 54). Zoology is the scientific study of animals, including pre-historic fossils.

Painted Rocks

WHAT YOU NEED:
- Small Rocks
- Acrylic Paint

Paint small rocks in bright colors. Varnish, then glue onto a shelf (see page 20).

1 Clean a small rock thoroughly.

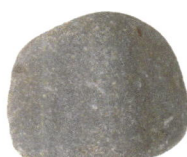

2 Paint with white to prime the surface.

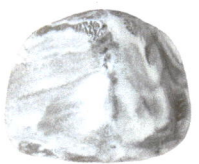

3 Paint with bright colors & varnish.

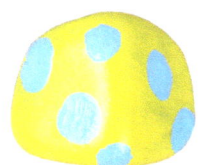

Apples and Crate

APPLES

WHAT YOU NEED:
- Several Plastic Beads
- Air-dry Clay
- 4 Regular Size Popsicle Sticks
- Two Jumbo Popsicle Sticks
- Acrylic Paint & Brush
- Toothpicks
- Sandpaper

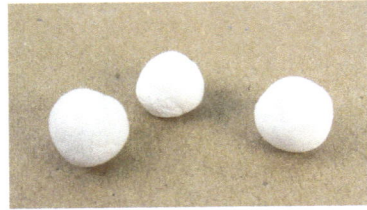

1 Start with small balls of clay the size of peas. Flatten them into disc shapes and cover the plastic beads with the clay. If you don't have beads, just use the clay balls by themselves.

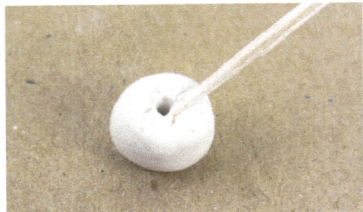

2 Find the hole in the center of a bead and stick a toothpick into it. With the tip of the toothpick press indents around the edge of the hole to form the top of the apple.

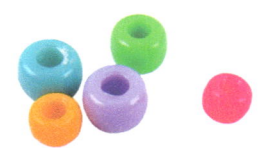

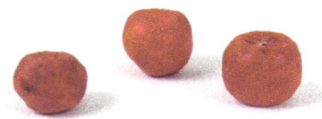

3 Complete the apples. Let the clay harden and then paint them red. Or green.

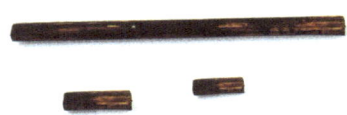

4 Color a toothpick brown with paint or a magic marker. Cut it into small pieces.

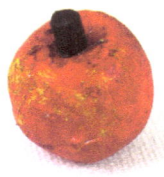

5 Stick the toothpick pieces into the holes in the apples to form the stems. Glue them in place. Varnish the apples.

CRATE

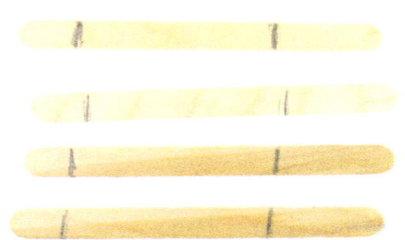

1 Measure a section about 2 1/4" on 4 regular size popsicle sticks. Use a wire cutter to cut off the excess ends. Smooth the rough ends with a piece of sandpaper.

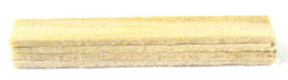

2 Glue the 4 sections together to make a block.

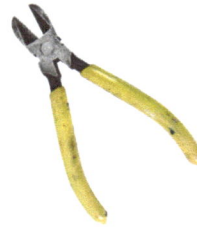

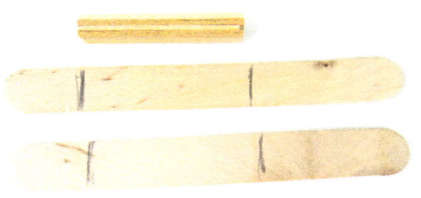

3 On two jumbo popsicle sticks measure 2 1/4". Cut them with a pair of scissors.

5 Cut two pieces from either the regular or jumbo sticks and glue to the sides of the crate.

4 Glue the two cut jumbo sticks to the block to form the front and back of the crate.

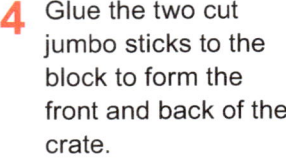

6 Paint with watery brown paint and wipe with a cloth while the paint is still damp to make the crate look old and worn. Glue on the apples. Apply a coat of varnish to finish.

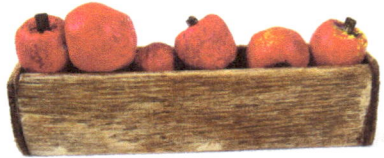

Monsters

WHAT YOU NEED:
- Air-dry Clay
- Wiggly Eyes
- Toothpicks & Paint

1 Flatten a ball of clay into a disc shape. Stand it up on one side and flatten the bottom so that it stands up on it's own.

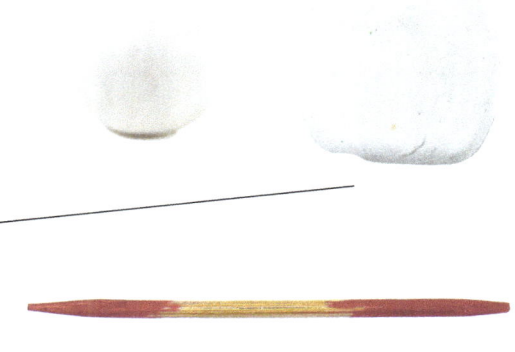

2 With a toothpick, poke two holes in the top for the horns. Let dry.

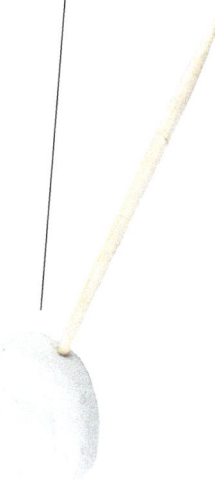

3 Paint both ends of a toothpick with a bright color.

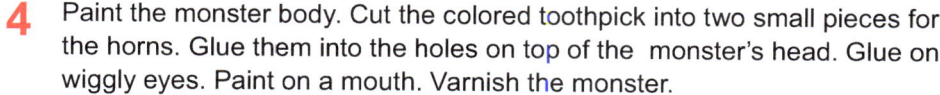

4 Paint the monster body. Cut the colored toothpick into two small pieces for the horns. Glue them into the holes on top of the monster's head. Glue on wiggly eyes. Paint on a mouth. Varnish the monster.

3/4"

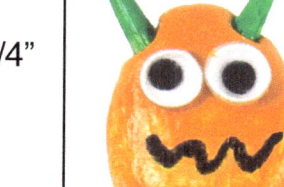
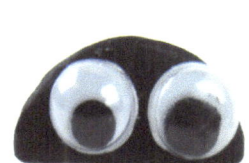
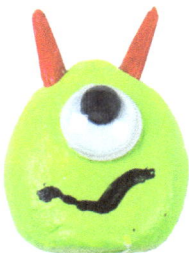
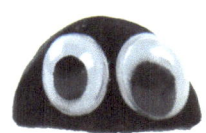

Vase of Flowers

WHAT YOU NEED:
- Miniature Flowers
- Wood Beads

1 Paint two wood beads with a matching color paint. Or you can use one larger bead instead. Any shape will work fine.

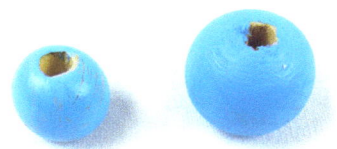

2 Twist the wire stems of the flowers together tightly.

3 Put glue on the end of the stems and thread them through the holes in the beads.

4 Cut off the stems at the bottom. Put glue in the hole at the bottom to seal the flowers inside beads.

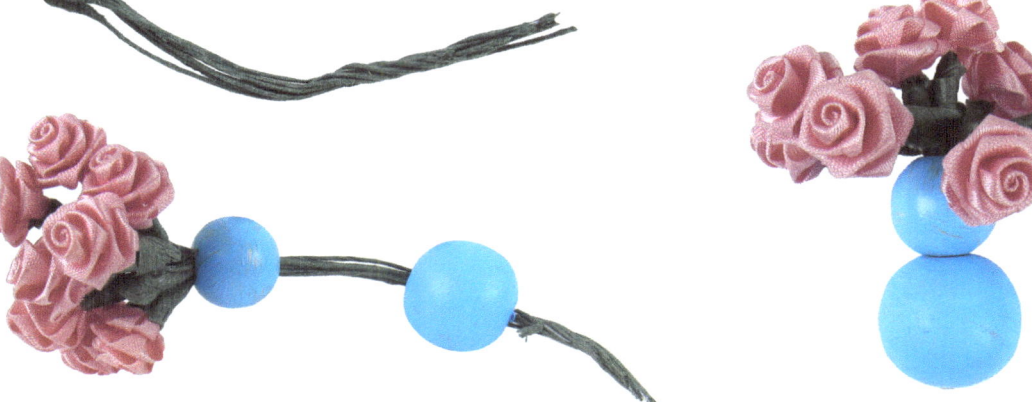

Halloween

PUMPKIN

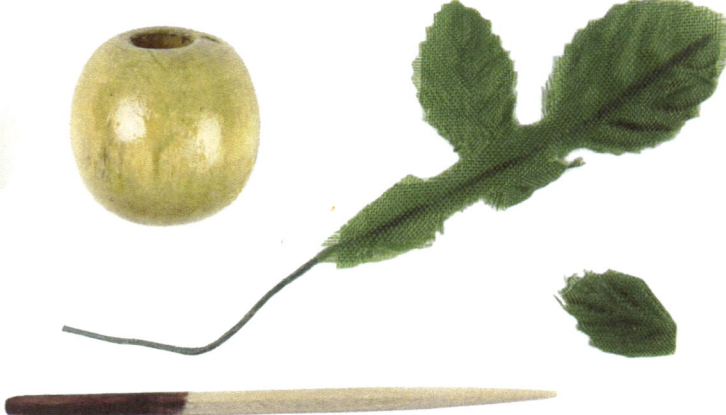

WHAT YOU NEED:
- Wooden Bead, Air-dry Clay
- Plastic or Silk Leaf
- Toothpicks
- Acrylic Paint & Mod Podge
- Tree Branch & Floral Wire

1 Flatten a clay ball and wrap it around the bead. Poke a hole in the center with the toothpick. Use the side of the toothpick to press indents into the sides of the clay from top to bottom to look like a pumpkin.

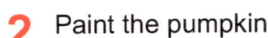

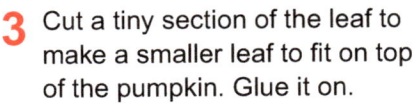

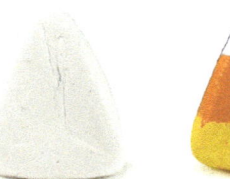

2 Paint the pumpkin.

3 Cut a tiny section of the leaf to make a smaller leaf to fit on top of the pumpkin. Glue it on.

4 Color a toothpick with brown paint or a brown magic marker. When dry, cut off a piece and stick it in the hole in the top of the pumpkin for the stem.

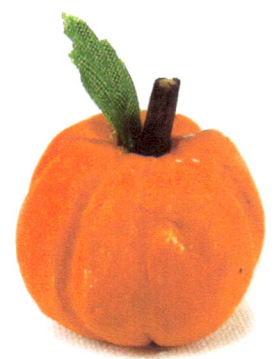

CANDY CORN

1 Shape a small ball of clay into a triangle. Let dry. Make several in different sizes.

2 Paint with white, orange and yellow stripes.

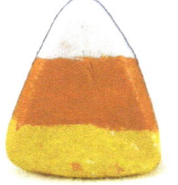

TREE

1 Wrap thin floral wire around all sections of a small branch.

2 Cover the wire with a coat of Mod Podge. Let dry.

3 Color the branch with black or brown paint.

4 Glue onto a popsicle stick shelf. See the Halloween project on page 29 for reference. All the ornaments look great when gathered together.

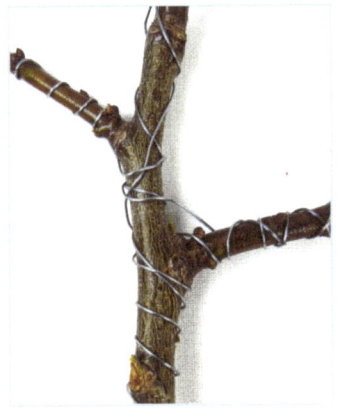

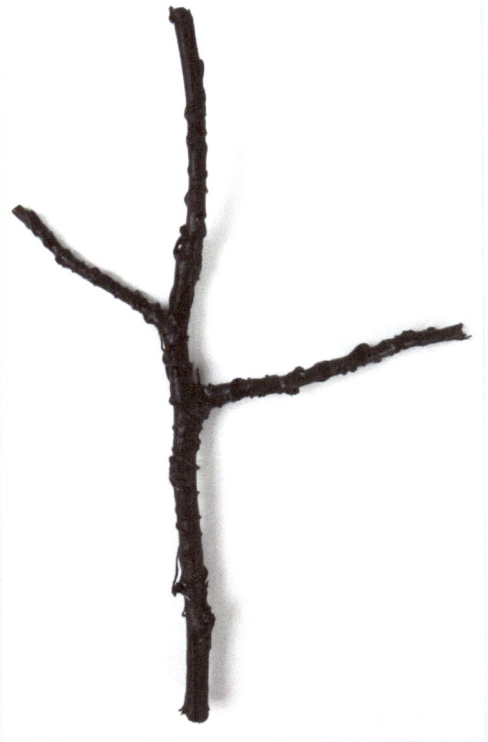

Snowman

WHAT YOU NEED:
- Air-dry Clay
- Toothpicks
- Jumbo Popsicle Sticks
- Acrylic Paint, Mod Podge or Varnish

1 Roll clay into three balls in three sizes. Stick them onto a toothpick with the smallest ball on the bottom.

3 Make two small boots out of two tiny logs of clay. Stick a toothpick in the top to make an opening in the boots. When dry, paint the boots red and glue them onto the legs on top.

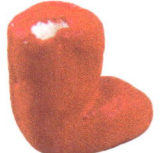

2 Trim the toothpick and cut it so it doesn't stick out of the top. Cut another toothpick into two small pieces and dab glue on the ends. Stick them into the large ball on top to form the legs.

Cut a tiny piece of toothpick for a carrot-shaped nose and color it orange. Put a dab of glue on the end and stick it into the middle of the face which is the smallest ball on the bottom. Let the clay harden overnight. Paint the snowman white.

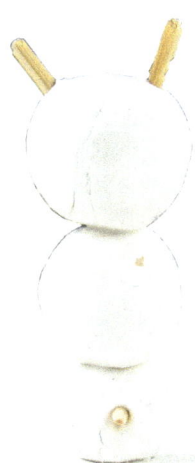

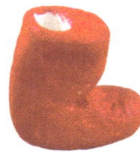

4 Glue two popsicle sticks together for a shelf (see page 14). Roll out a long, skinny log of clay the length of the sticks.

6 Add eyes and a mouth with a marker or a tiny brush and black paint. Add buttons. Glue two small pieces of brown-colored toothpick or wire to the sides to form arms. Glue on small snowballs on either side of the snowman. Paint the snow with white, then coat with varnish or Mod Podge to bond all the pieces firmly together. Glue this shelf to a finished alphabet plaque (see page 20).

5 Cover one side of the sticks with glue and flatten the log of clay along the top to create snow drifts. Press the clay down with your fingertips to spread out the clay. Make the drifts uneven. Put glue on top of the head of the snowman and push it down into the clay snow so it stands on its own upside-down. Let the clay harden. Apply Mod Podge or varnish around the base of the head with a small brush to hold it firmly in place.

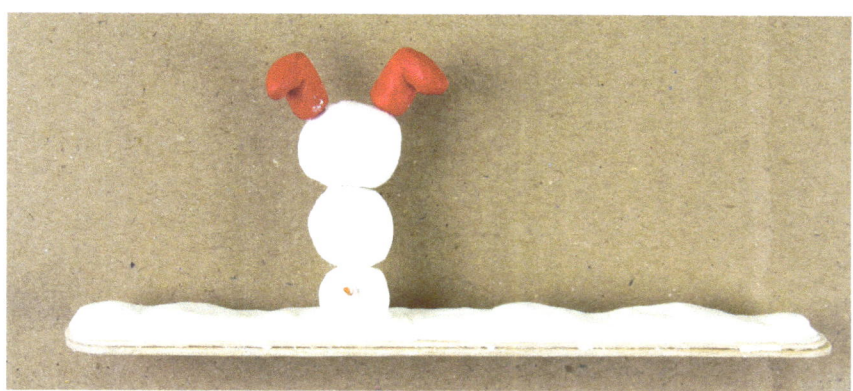

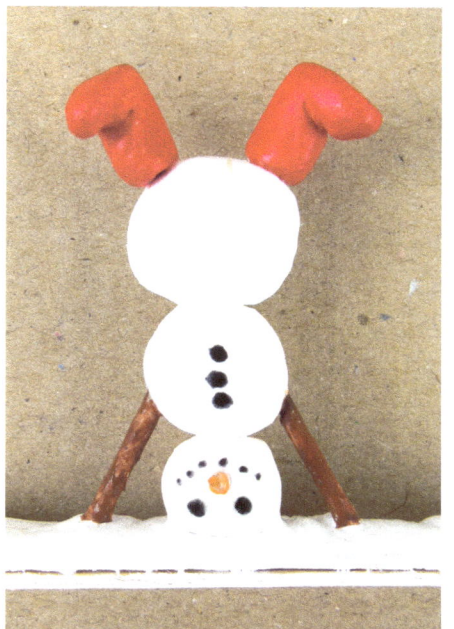

Buttons

WHAT YOU NEED:
- Wooden Bead
- Air-dry Clay

You can find all kinds of fun buttons at a craft store that can be easily turned into ornaments. Here's how: Snip the button loop off the back. Glue button to a bead to make the button stand up straight. Glue onto a shelf.

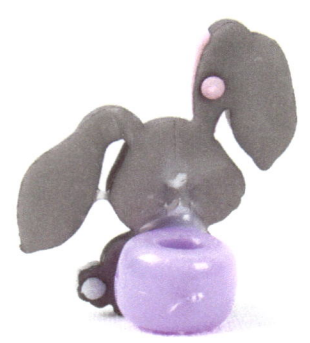

Animal Buttons on page 44

Stickers

WHAT YOU NEED:
- Stickers
- Air-dry Clay

Sometimes all you have on hand to decorate your Wildstyle popsicle stick projects are stickers. No problem. You can turn flat stickers into three-dimensional ornaments with this simple trick: If the sticker is flimsy stick it onto cardstock and cut it out. Take a small ball of air-dry clay and mold it to fit on the back of the sticker. Remove and spread glue on the back. Put the clay back on and paint it when dry.

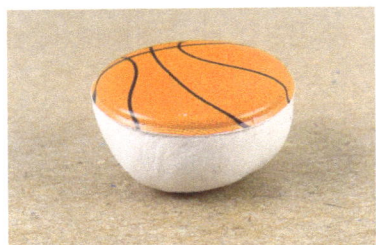

Basketball sticker - side view

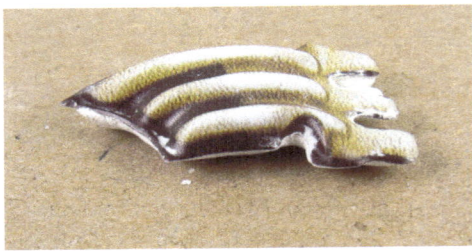

Dinosaur bone sticker - front and back

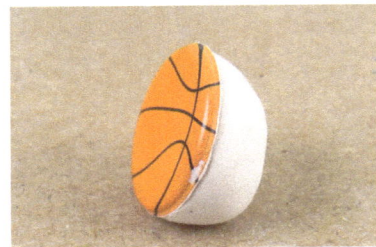

Basketball sticker on page 36

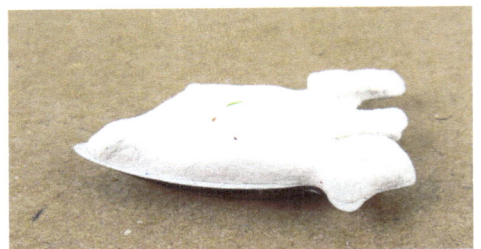

Dinosaur bone stickers on page 47

Keyboard

WHAT YOU NEED:
- Photocopy of Paper Keyboard below
- Jumbo Popsicle Stick

*If you can't make a photocopy just draw a keyboard on a stick.

To make a keyboard:
Make a photocopy of the Keyboard below. Glue a jumbo stick onto the back of the paper Keyboard. Cut out and trim edges.

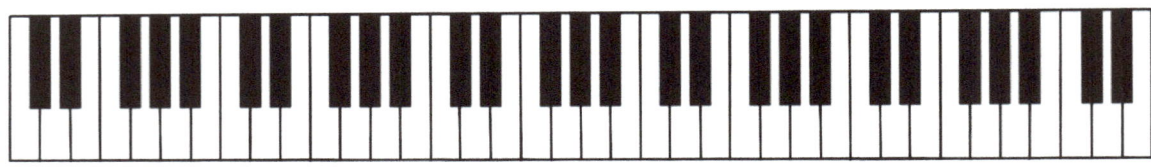

MAKE A PHOTOCOPY

Use this popsicle stick keyboard to make a shelf for your project (see page 20).

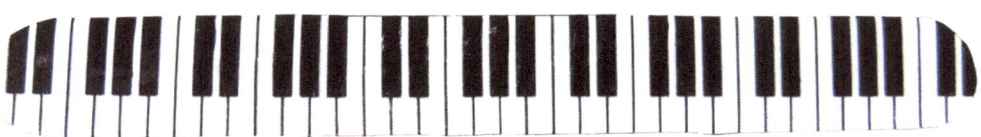

FINISHED POPSICLE STICK KEYBOARD

Zylophone

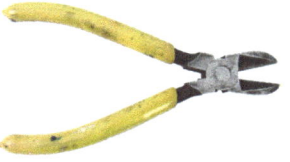

WHAT YOU NEED:
- 10 Regular Size Popsicle Sticks
- Air-dry Clay
- Acrylic Paint
- Masking Tape
- Wood Barbecue Skewer
- Sandpaper

To cut popsicle sticks you need a wire cutter or a very sharp pair of scissors

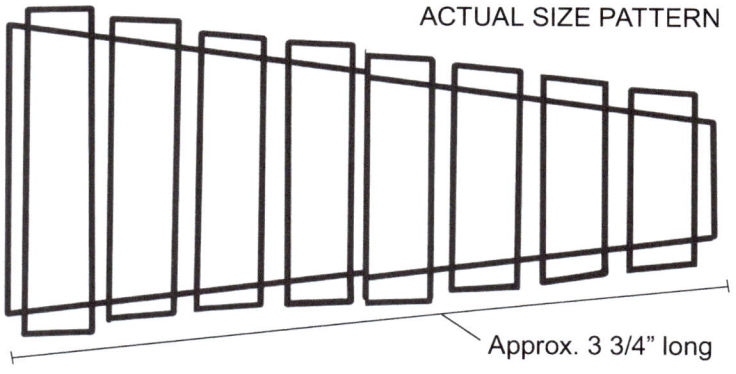

ACTUAL SIZE PATTERN

Approx. 3 3/4" long

1 On two popsicle sticks, mark off a section about 3 3/4" with a pencil.

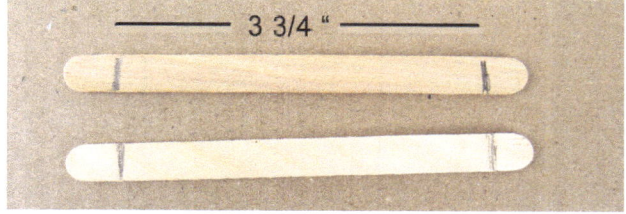

3 3/4 "

2 Cut off the ends at the lines. Smooth the ends with a small piece of sandpaper.

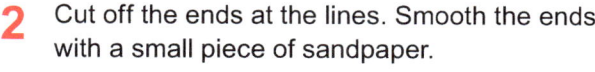

3 Place three pieces of masking tape on a piece of paper or cardboard like this:

Sticky side down   Sticky side up   Sticky side down

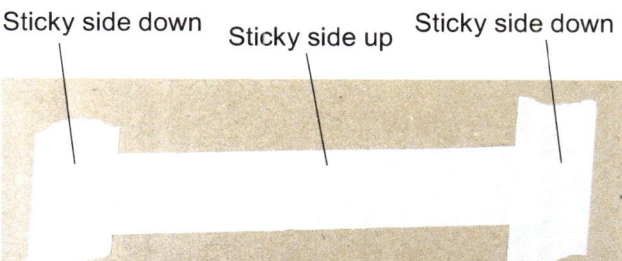

4 Cut small pieces of popsicle sticks using the pattern at the top of this page as a guide. Stick them down on to the tape, largest to smallest.

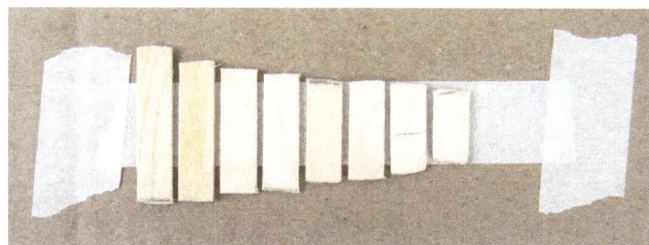

5 Glue the two 3 3/4" sticks onto the smaller sticks standing up to form a base for the Xylophone. Let dry and then remove from tape. Rub a small piece of sandpaper all around the sticks to make all edges smooth.

6 Color with acrylic paint, water-color paint, colored pencils or markers.

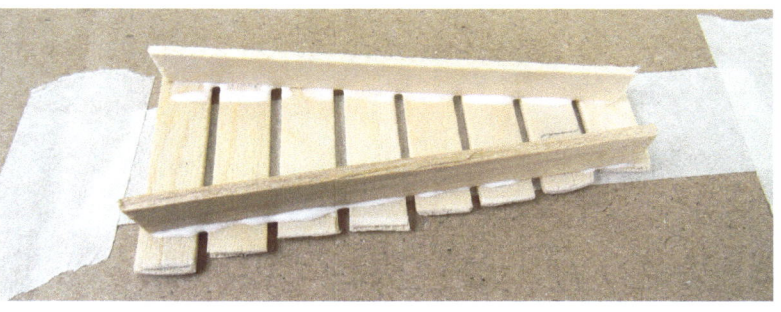

1 Mallets: Cut two pieces 2" long from a wooden barbecue skewer or round craft stick. Roll two small balls of air-dry clay.

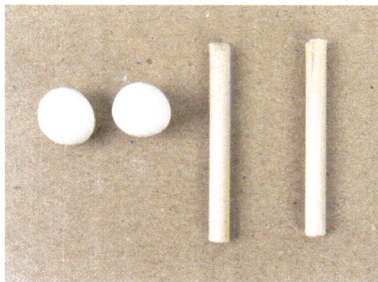

2 Push the clay balls onto the tops of the sticks. Round them out with your fingertips. Let dry, paint and varnish.

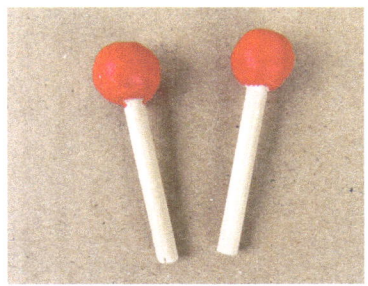